# The Trojan War

*An Enthralling Overview of a Legendary Conflict of Ancient Greece and Its Role in History and Greek Mythology*

© Copyright 2021

All Rights Reserved. No part of this book may be reproduced in any form without permission in writing from the author. Reviewers may quote brief passages in reviews.

Disclaimer: No part of this publication may be reproduced or transmitted in any form or by any means, mechanical or electronic, including photocopying or recording, or by any information storage and retrieval system, or transmitted by email without permission in writing from the publisher.

While all attempts have been made to verify the information provided in this publication, neither the author nor the publisher assumes any responsibility for errors, omissions, or contrary interpretations of the subject matter herein.

This book is for entertainment purposes only. The views expressed are those of the author alone, and should not be taken as expert instruction or commands. The reader is responsible for his or her own actions.

Adherence to all applicable laws and regulations, including international, federal, state, and local laws governing professional licensing, business practices, advertising, and all other aspects of doing business in the US, Canada, UK, or any other jurisdiction is the sole responsibility of the purchaser or reader.

Neither the author nor the publisher assumes any responsibility or liability whatsoever on the behalf of the purchaser or reader of these materials. Any perceived slight of any individual or organization is purely unintentional.

# Free limited time bonus

Stop for a moment. We have a free bonus set up for you. The problem is this: we forget 90% of everything that we read after 7 days. Crazy fact, right? Here's the solution: we've created a printable, 1-page pdf summary for this book that you're reading now. All you have to do to get your free pdf summary is to go to the following website: **https://livetolearn.lpages.co/enthrallinghistory/**

Once you do, it will be intuitive. Enjoy, and thank you!

# Contents

INTRODUCTION ............................................................................................. 1
PART ONE: BEFORE THE WAR ..................................................................... 4
CHAPTER 1: WHO WERE THE TROJANS? ................................................. 5
CHAPTER 2: WHO WERE THE ACHAEANS? ........................................... 11
CHAPTER 3: CAUSES OF THE TROJAN WAR .......................................... 17
CHAPTER 4: GATHERING OF THE ACHAEAN FORCES ....................... 22
PART TWO: THE TROJAN WAR ................................................................. 28
CHAPTER 5: THE WAR BEGINS ................................................................ 29
CHAPTER 6: THE ILIAD ............................................................................. 34
CHAPTER 7: THE DEATHS OF PENTHESILEA, MEMNON, AND ACHILLES ..................................................................................................... 43
CHAPTER 8: AJAX'S DEATH AND THE LAST PROPHECIES ................. 51
CHAPTER 9: THE TROJAN HORSE AND THE SACK OF TROY ............ 58
PART THREE: THE IMPACT OF THE TROJAN WAR ............................... 72
CHAPTER 10: THE LITERATURE: ANCIENT GREEK WRITERS ON THE TROJAN WAR ............................................................................... 73
CHAPTER 11: THE LEGEND: HOW ANCIENT GREEKS VIEWED THE TROJAN WAR ...................................................................................... 85
CHAPTER 12: THE LEGACY: MODERN-DAY FINDINGS AND INTERPRETATIONS .................................................................................... 97
CONCLUSION ............................................................................................ 107

**HERE'S ANOTHER BOOK BY ENTHRALLING HISTORY THAT YOU MIGHT LIKE**.................................................................109
**FREE LIMITED TIME BONUS**..................................................................110
**REFERENCES** ..........................................................................................111

# Introduction

The Trojan War: epic story or historical fact? Historians disagree.

Sometime around the year 1200 BCE, a decade-long war raged between the ancient Greeks and their rivals in Troy across the Aegean Sea. The story is among the oldest in the world, and the account written by a Greek poet named Homer still makes it into many high school and university curricula. Who were these Greeks, and what drove them to fight for so long, so far from home? Who were the Trojans, and how were they able to fend off the mighty Greeks for ten long years? Perhaps even more important, what has caused us to tell and retell this story for thousands of years?

Up until the mid-18th century, it was widely held that the Trojan War was a pure myth, but there have always been a few who held that the human side of the story was true. Archeologists have discovered the remains of a city they believe to be Troy's Ancient Bronze Age city, dating back to the 12th century BCE. Evidence includes scattered skeletons and charred debris, indicating the city was destroyed during wartime. Excavations in 1988 revealed a large city (75 acres worth!) surrounded by wheat fields – a city apparently in its heyday. But was this Homer's "Troy"?

Hittite texts close to the period show that the city Homer called Troy was referred to as "Wilusa" – which is rendered "Ilion" in Greek – the language in which Homer wrote. This points to a connection between "Ilion" and the *Iliad*.

There is little doubt that Homer's story is full of mythological gods who could not have possibly engaged in an *actual* battle, but the fly in the ointment does not render the ointment imaginary; it simply *enhances* it. To understand the *Iliad*, we must consider the time in which it was written.

In the middle of the $8^{th}$ century BCE, Greece was just coming out of its Dark Ages and saw the reintroduction of written language – something that had been lost. People believed that gods and goddesses played a part in their daily lives and that judgment and fate depended on their worthiness in these gods' eyes. As city-states were on the rise and colonies were being founded within – and outside of – the usual Grecian boundaries, the first notions of classical philosophy were taking hold. These, among other developments, led to a more thoughtful sort of nationalism, and Homer's story was thought to have united weary citizens in a frenzy of patriotism that had been all but lost to the prior centuries.

Great timing for Homer! Dictating the *Iliad* (Homer was blind), he wove mythology in with history, calling his listeners and readers to consider one's morals and choices rather than only victories and losses. Plato would later proclaim that Homer was "the educator of all Greece" for the impact Homer's works had on Greece at that time. And surely, this formative text for the ancient Greeks has had a longstanding effect even dozens of centuries after it was written.

Join us as we look at the background and setting for the Trojan War of Homer's *Iliad* and learn yet another lesson of the futility and folly of warfare. Why did it start? Why did it escalate? What can we learn from this war – mythical or not – today? Much like the historical and mythological source material, the answers to those questions will be interwoven with the actions and politics of the Greek gods. Read on...

# PART ONE: BEFORE THE WAR

# Chapter 1: Who Were the Trojans?

The city of Troy is found in Turkey, called *Anatolia* in the time of the Trojans of yore. For modern reference, the ruins of the ancient city are located near the city of Gallipoli.

*Approximate location of Troy. Credit: https://www.google.com/maps/place/Gallipoli+Peninsula/@42.7867119,22.0686044,5z/)*

There has been much debate about the heritage of the Trojans. While the invading Greeks were a group from the mainland called the Achaeans, there were plenty of Greek city-states on the other side of the Aegean as well. Given that most stories of the war told by the Greeks paint the Trojans in an equal or even superior light to that of the Achaeans, it was long believed that they were Greek themselves.

However, recent excavations have changed most archaeologists' minds and vindicated the account of Homer and other early Greek historians. Troy's original identification and excavation took place between 1863 and 1890 when Frank Calvert and Heinrich Schliemann uncovered a much less impressive site than scholars were hoping for. A small citadel of about an acre was unearthed, leading to the opinion that Troy must have been far past its prime when the Achaeans invaded and defeated them.

But recent excavations led by Manfred Osman Korfmann have benefitted from both a century of scrutiny and new technologies that have allowed his team to reveal a Troy worthy of the epic story we have come to know. Instead of less than one acre, Troy was a sprawling and fortified seventy-five acres that would have been in the glittering prime of its influence and culture, just as Homer described it. Well, maybe not just as described by Homer, given his penchant for weaving in the interfering nature of the Greek gods and goddesses, but much closer than archaeologists had formerly believed.

These excavations have revealed not only the power and wealth of the Trojans at the time of the war with the Achaeans and their Anatolian heritage. The city planning, buildings, and art were all more consistent with those of southwestern Asia than southeastern Europe. Documents were discovered that linked their language to that of the Hittites of Palestine and provided evidence that they were an ally of Troy. While plenty of Greek influence was found, it was not dominant, and it was much more likely to have been the result of trade and cultural interaction rather than cultural relation.

Given that recent excavations have corroborated much of what Homer and Greek historians have claimed, perhaps more credence can be given to the description of the Trojans provided by their stories. Even Homer's descriptions of the gods and goddesses, once seen at best as pure entertainment and at worst a blight on an otherwise historical record, have begun to receive more attention. That is because once we accept the significant archaeological evidence indicating that Troy was not a Greek city, we are left with the uncomfortable situation of the Trojans worshiping and being aided by certain Greek deities.

Did the Greeks import their gods from the Near East, much like the Romans reappropriated and renamed them centuries later? Or, perhaps, there was simply some overlap. The biggest mystery centers around the role of Apollo, who is credited with building Troy's famous walls that kept the Greeks out for so long. As a character in Homer's tale, he takes the side of the Trojans at key points, beginning with a plague he set loose in the Greek encampment and by guiding the poisoned arrow that ultimately killed the seemingly invulnerable Greek warrior, Achilles.

What is more, Princess Cassandra of Troy was a priestess of Apollo, and her brother Hector, the chief Trojan hero of the tale, was rumored to have been fathered by Apollo. So, if the Trojans were not Greek, what is a Greek god doing so entwined in their culture?

### The Significance of Apollo

According to Greek mythology, Apollo was the son of Zeus and Leto, who was a daughter of the Titans that Zeus and his sibling gods overthrew. The fact that there exists an old set of gods that were ousted has long been interpreted to indicate an early struggle of the Greeks against non-Greek leaders for autonomy.

After trapping most of the Titans in Tartarus, Zeus took Hera as his wife, but Leto was the daughter of his former enemies. Even the name Leto has Lydian origins rather than Greek origins, and many temples in her honor have been found across Anatolia. Further, it is important to note that the *Iliad* was written by Homer about four hundred years after the events of the Trojan War, which would have been more than enough time for Leto, Apollo, and his twin sister Artemis to be incorporated into the Greek pantheon. Due to the significance of the war and the Greek victory, Apollo and Artemis were promoted to Mt. Olympus, making them among the most important of their deities.

More evidence of the adoption of Apollo by the Greeks only after the war includes the sheer variety of his powers and gifts. He is the god of the sun, even though the Greeks already had the Titan Helios filling that role. Apollo would drive a ball of fire around the sky each day behind his chariot. He is also the god of light, art, archery, music, plagues, healing, prophecy, and truth, to name just a few. These are arguably more impressive than Zeus himself and are the hallmarks of a more significant deity than his supporting roles in Greek mythology would indicate.

### The Royal Family of Troy

The Trojans involved in the tale were mostly the members of the royal family. Like their Greek opponents, Troy governed through a monarchy, at the head of which stood King Priam when the Achaeans stormed across the Aegean Sea to lay siege to their gates for the second time. Yes, *the second time.*

The first time was during the reign of Priam's father, Laomedon. Laomedon made two very famous mistakes for which his people and family would pay dearly. First, he refused payment to Apollo and Poseidon after they had helped to build his city's walls. As punishment, the former unleashed a pestilence upon the city, and the latter set loose a monster called a Cetus to attack it from the sea. It took the efforts of the famous Greek demi-god Heracles to slay the beast and end the plague, but Laomedon made his second and last mistake of refusing to give Heracles the horses that he was promised in exchange for his aid.

Unlike the ten-year campaign that came later, Heracles and his companion, Telamon, made short work of the siege. Telamon's father had helped to construct a part of the wall, and unlike the portions made by Apollo and Poseidon, this part had a weakness. The warriors exploited this secret knowledge to enter the city and kill King Laomedon. As part of their revenge for the dead king's treachery, they set themselves to murdering his sons one by one until they reached young Priam. His sister, Hesione, offered herself as ransom to Telamon, who took her as his wife in return for sparing Priam. In fact, Priam means "the ransomed" (and prior to these events, he had been known as *Podarces*).

Priam ascended to the Trojan throne, and by all accounts, he was a fair and wise leader. Troy prospered under his rule, and he is said to have fathered as many as eighty-six children. In keeping with Trojan custom for aristocratic men, he had many wives – the primary of whom was Hecuba. Hecuba herself gave birth to a staggering nineteen children, among whom were Hector, Paris, and Cassandra, all of whom played significant roles in the Trojan War. Hector was the heir apparent to the throne and the strongest of all the Trojan warriors, even more than his father Priam. Hector was seen as the best that Troy had to offer. Even the Greeks (who were responsible for telling the story) portrayed him as the most heroic of all its characters. Homer's *Iliad* is as much about the tragedy of Hector as it is about the rage of Achilles. Through Homer's work, Hector and his wife Andromache represent both Trojan and Greek ideals for men and women in their societies.

Paris, Hector's brother, is a different story, though, and in some accounts, he is thought to be the son of the god Apollo. While Hector is seen as Troy's greatest defender, Paris is responsible for putting the city in danger. Throughout the story, the contrast between the two brothers is continually highlighted. Where Hector is skilled in the arts of warfare, Paris admits his shortcomings and primarily uses a bow and arrow to avoid close combat. When challenged by the Spartan

King Menelaus to single combat to end the war, Paris flees rather than accept his defeat, leading to the deaths of many more Trojans and Greeks. In contrast, Hector is willing to die in defense of the city and his family's honor, which he demonstrates many times over.

Cassandra, daughter of Priam and Hecuba, is another important figure in the events of the Trojan War. As a priestess of Apollo, the god came to her and offered her the gift of prophecy. When she later refused to father his children, Apollo cursed her, telling her that all of her accurate prophecies would always be met with utter disbelief. As a result, she predicted the fall of Troy to the Achaeans, but *no one listened*. This bit of story adds more to the confusion surrounding the role of Apollo, who alternatingly supported and cursed the Trojans. The "Cassandra Syndrome" has made its way into popular culture, referring to anyone who makes valid and prudent warnings that go ignored.

Finally, there is the character Aeneas, who plays only a minor role in the Trojan War but a far greater one in the events that followed. He was the son of a Trojan prince and the goddess Aphrodite, and he is one of the few Trojans to escape slavery or death after the burning of the city by the victorious Greeks. The gods commanded him to flee along with his father, son, and several companions. His story is described by Virgil (a popular Roman poet) in the *Aeneid*, which details his adventures leading up to his relocation to Italy and his connection to Romulus and Remus, the first kings of Rome. In many ways, his tale mirrors that of Odysseus – Ithaca's king and the central figure in the *Odyssey* – and the Greeks attempting to return to Ithaca following the long war.

# Chapter 2: Who Were the Achaeans?

The Greeks involved in the Trojan War were part of *Mycenaean Greece*, which lasted from about 1750 BCE until 1050 BCE.

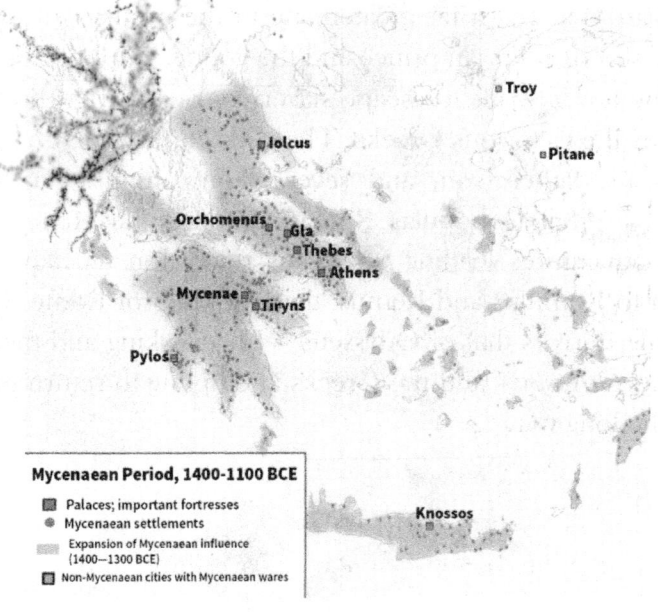

*Mycenaean Greece. Credit: https://en.wikipedia.org/wiki/File:Mycenaean_World_en.png.*

Homer refers to these Greeks most commonly as the "Achaeans" in the *Iliad*, and the same convention will be repeated here. However, it should be noted that this is somewhat confusing since the term technically refers to people from the area called Achaea in the northern Peloponnesian Peninsula, and the Achaean League was formed in the third century BCE among the city-states of the region. Homer's Achaeans were not restricted to this region and instead came from kingdoms across the Greek mainland. Homer also refers to the Greek forces as Danaans, Argives, Panhellenes, and Hellenes in the *Iliad*. Again, for the purposes of our discussion, we will use the collective name for these people: "Achaeans."

In many ways, these Achaeans were the Vikings of the Mediterranean during the Bronze Age. They had not yet matured into the classical civilization of Athens during its Golden Age – nor even the structured warrior society of Sparta during the Persian Wars. These Greek civilizations were less powerful but perhaps more menacing than their descendants would be.

In some of the first warships ever built, they fanned out through the islands of the Aegean Sea and took what they could, spreading their culture, goods, language, and a fair amount of death as they went. Still, they were not mere brutes, and their shipbuilding was also used to bolster their economy through trade with neighbors such as Egypt and Assyria. Linguistic analyses, archaeological evidence, and genetic studies indicate that the Achaeans themselves were probably descendants of indigenous Greeks, Minoans from Crete, and one or several Indo-European tribes that settled the area after migrating through the Caucasus.

### Agamemnon and Menelaus

Like their Trojan rivals, powerful Achaean city-states were protected by walls since they often warred with one another, and the Greek habit of building citadels upon a hilltop called an acropolis can be traced back to this time period.

*Depiction of an acropolis. Credit: Wikimedia Commons.*

The largest of these city-states was called *Mycenae* in northeastern Peloponnese near modern-day Mykines. At its peak around 1350 BCE, it had a population of about 30,000 people and was nearly three times larger than its closest Greek rivals and erstwhile allies. Before the Trojan War, the leader of Mycenae was King Atreus. He and his wife, Aerope, had two sons, Agamemnon and Menelaus.

Agamemnon was the heir to the throne, but the family was thrown into chaos when Atreus discovered that Aerope had committed adultery with his brother, Thyestes. Enraged, Atreus not only killed the sons of Thyestes but forced him to eat them. Afterward, Thyestes fathered a new son named Aegisthus through incest with his daughter, Pelopia. Aegisthus grew to adulthood and took revenge for his father, murdering Atreus and installing Thyestes to the throne of Mycenae.

Since the throne had been taken from Agamemnon, he and Menelaus fled. They were given refuge in Sparta by King Tyndareus, who saw the two as innocent amidst all the madness of their family. There, they met Tyndareus's daughter, Helen. News of Helen's beauty had already spread throughout all of the kingdoms, and powerful suitors came from all across Greece with lavish gifts to compete for her hand in marriage. As a woman in her time, place, and social standing, Helen had no choice in the matter of marriage; that job fell to her father, but he feared that doing so would start a war.

Odysseus (one of the suitors) had a clever idea for the king: require all suitors to swear an oath to uphold the final decision *before it was made*. Each quickly agreed since this would ensure the people's support if they were the one selected to marry Helen. Tyndareus selected Menelaus, and all of the suitors left peacefully, except for Odysseus. He had not given his advice for free; in exchange, he requested Tyndareus's support in his courtship of Helen's cousin Penelope, with whom he had fallen in love during his visit.

Agamemnon also married a daughter of Tyndareus named Clytemnestra, but it was Menelaus who ascended the throne upon the king's death because of his marriage to Helen, as he was the elder of the two. Agamemnon's ambition had led him to seek Helen's hand, but he was bound now by his oath to support both his brother's marriage and his new throne. Still seeing an opportunity, he convinced Menelaus to help him take back Mycenae from Thyestes. They marched north and surprised their uncle, chasing him and his son from the city and installing Agamemnon as the most powerful man in Achaean Greece.

## Achaean Heroes of the Trojan War

Agamemnon, Menelaus, and Odysseus would all take part in the Trojan War, leading their kingdoms into battle. After departing from Sparta with Penelope, Odysseus soon took the throne from his father, becoming the king of Ithaca. His plan to gain Tyndareus's support for marrying Penelope was no fluke; the idea was carefully crafted. Odysseus is regarded as one of the cleverest protagonists in Greek history and mythology, preferring to outwit his opponents rather than overpower them. This characteristic lies in stark contrast to the Achaean warrior Achilles, who was brash, hot-tempered, and depended on his world-famous prowess in battle to settle disputes.

Odysseus and Nestor (the king of Pylos) became primarily responsible for recruiting and uniting the Achaean kingdoms against Troy in an effort to begin the war. Like Priam, all of Nestor's brothers were killed by Heracles, a Greek demi-god. By the time of the Trojan War, Nestor was an old man – about 70 years old – with a penchant for inspiring others through tales of his heroic youth.

One person that required very little persuasion was Diomedes, king of Argos. According to legend, he was the son of Ares and a favorite of Athena because of the warrior goddess's respect for his skill in battle. He was considered second only to Achilles among the Achaean forces in this regard and had seen more fighting in his young years than even the elderly Nestor. Among all the Achaean heroes, only he and Odysseus were praised in the *Iliad* for their cunning and strategy, making him the complete package. Diomedes later became the king of Argos and founded several cities in Italy, where he became fully deified and worshiped after his death.

Another demi-god on the Achaeans' roster was Ajax the Great, son of King Telamon of Salamis. Homer and others portray Ajax the Great as a courageous and towering figure for the Greeks. He twice fought Hector to a draw, leading to a budding respect between the opposing heroes. There was another Ajax in their ranks as well, called Ajax the Lesser (or sometimes Locrian Ajax) to better distinguish between the two. Neither were kings, but they led their forces from Salamis and Locris, respectively, in the siege of Troy.

Commanding the Cretan armies (whose archers were considered among the best "light missile" troops in the ancient world) was King Idomeneus, a grandson of King Minos of minotaur fame. Over the course of the war, he became one of Agamemnon's most trusted advisors and was among the Achaean warriors who infiltrated Troy's walls by hiding inside of the giant wooden horse as part of the scheme concocted by Odysseus. Another warrior within the walls of the Trojan horse was the Athenian king, Menestheus. Like Diomedes, he knew much of the tactics in war but was often criticized for being less valiant and skilled when it came to his own fighting.

Nearly all of these Achaean heroes were among the suitors of Helen of Sparta and were bound by the oath they gave to support Menelaus. Odysseus's trick may have allowed for a peaceful resolution to the competition for Helen, but when the young prince of Troy absconded with the queen to name her Helen of Troy, they were all ensnared by their honor.

*While some painters believe Helen and Paris were in love, most depict Helen's abduction in a violent manner. This one is aptly named* The Abduction of Helen, *and it is by Francesco Primaticcio. Credit: Wikimedia Commons.*

# Chapter 3: Causes of the Trojan War

In this chapter, we will talk about the events that led up to the Trojan War, like the Apple of Discord, the Judgement of Paris, and the abduction of Helen. We will not discuss the details of the war just yet, but rather set the foundations for a better understanding of the causes.

Many believe that the Trojan War began when Paris kidnapped Helen of Sparta – or the more romantic view: they fell in love and ran away together. The truth of it may be lost to time, and both versions of the story have their merits. Either way, Menelaus was able to rally many of his fellow kings and warriors to launch a thousand ships (sound familiar?) across the Aegean Sea to lay war at the gates of Troy. But like all tales of the ancient Greeks, it is a little more complicated than that.

The seeds for the conflict were planted in both a prophecy and a contest, each involving the gods and goddesses of Mt. Olympus. The prophecy in question was given to the god Zeus and his brother Poseidon, each who had fallen in love with the beautiful sea-nymph named Thetis. They received a prophecy that Thetis' son would rise up to destroy his father, wielding powers untold if he were to be sired by the likes of Zeus or Poseidon. The pair of gods backed off, and

Zeus instead decreed that Thetis must marry the elderly King Peleus of Phthia. Zeus had always feared that he would one day be dethroned by his offspring, much the way that he and his siblings and rebelled to defeat their Titan parents. He began to concoct a plan for a war to depopulate the earth of many of the demi-god children running about.

*Sea nymph Thetis as depicted on a black-figure dish. Credit: https://en.wikipedia.org/wiki/Thetis.*

## The Judgment of Paris

After the wedding of Thetis and Peleus, Zeus organized a huge feast in celebration, but did not invite Eris, the goddess of strife and discord. To sow her revenge – and live up to her name – she tossed a golden apple amid the revelers, with the inscription "To the fairest" engraved upon it. Hera, Athena, and Aphrodite all claimed the golden apple as *obviously* their own, and to settle the dispute, Zeus sent them to Paris of Troy, naming Paris as the deciding judge.

Golden Apple of Discord *by Jacob Jordaens. Credit: Wikimedia Commons.*

Each goddess attempted to bribe Paris in accordance with their nature. Hera, Zeus' wife and the Queen of the Gods, offered Paris immense power, promising to make him the king of Europa and Asia. The Goddess of Wisdom and War, Athena, told Paris that she would grant him great wisdom and skill in battle if he selected her. Lastly, Aphrodite, the Goddess of Love and Beauty, told Paris that if he chose her, he would fall in love with the most beautiful woman in the world.

Paris chose Aphrodite, and thus fell prey to Zeus' trap, as Helen of Sparta held the title – as she was already betrothed to King Menelaus.

Paris has often been vilified or deemed a coward for his choices, but in this contest, there was no winning. No matter whom he chose, he was making two powerful enemies for Troy who would end up supporting the Greeks in the war to come.

Regardless, after being shown the likeness of Helen by Aphrodite, Paris set sail to Sparta on a diplomatic mission with the ulterior motive of abducting her. To make good on her word, Aphrodite sent Eros (in Roman mythology, Cupid) to shoot an enchanted arrow at Helen just before greeting Paris. When she looked up to see him, she fell in love and agreed to elope and run away with him to the grand citadel of Troy. Other versions claim that Helen was taken against her will; this version was certainly the angle that Menelaus used to convince his fellow Greeks to go to war.

The Love of Helen and Paris *by Jacques-Louis David.* Credit: *Wikimedia Commons.*

## The Road to War

When Paris and Helen arrived in Troy, the royal family was furious – especially Priam and Hector, who understood that the Greeks would not simply allow this to go unpunished, and that war with Greece was likely inevitable. Menelaus and Odysseus journeyed to Troy to negotiate Helen's release, but Paris (and quite possibly

Helen) would not agree to the queen's return. Bound by their own duty to their son and brother, respectively, King Priam and Prince Hector agreed to let Helen stay in their city, turning the Greek emissaries away.

The next time they would see them, the Greeks would arrive with one of the largest armadas that had ever been assembled. Having turned down Hera, Paris and the Trojans would not see their prosperity last and would not become the lords of Europe and Asia. And having turned down Athena, it would be the Greeks who boasted the bold strategies of Odysseus – and who had the greatest warrior of all in Achilles. For a time, though, Paris had Helen of Troy.

To more completely understand the causes of the Trojan War, it is important to take a step back from the myths and look at the context of the Aegean world in the late Bronze Age. While Troy was a Greek rival, the Hittites of Anatolia were likely a Greek enemy. Troy's fortress protected Hittite affluence, a people who remained independent but were in constant threat of being swallowed up by both of its neighboring powers.

While mentions of the Hittites are frustratingly absent from Homer's account of the war in the *Iliad*, it's theorized that perhaps Homer used an unrecognized name to refer to them when counting the allies of Troy. Knowing the power and influence of the Bronze Age Hittites in Anatolia, this would make more sense than leaving them out altogether, and closer relations between the Trojans and the Hittites would have been enough to make the Greeks start worrying about the safety of their own city-states in Anatolia. For as long as Troy remained neutral, they had remained safe. Either through miscalculation, misguided strategies, or personal grudges, the Trojans seemed to be turning away from the Greeks, who may have preferred *no Troy at all* over and *enemy Troy*.

# Chapter 4: Gathering of the Achaean Forces

Once diplomacy failed to retrieve Helen, Menelaus began recruiting others to his cause. His first stop was Mycenae and his brother, Agamemnon, who agreed to come – only if he would be the commander-in-chief of all the Greek forces on the expedition. Knowing that he needed the might his brother controlled, Menelaus agreed. Yet, alone, their two kingdoms would not be enough.

Adding to the drama, even before the Greeks could leave Aulis for Troy, the city was hit by a plague and forced to remain in port due to an absence of wind. Per myth, Artemis (Goddess of the Hunt) required a sacrifice be made: Agamemnon's daughter, Iphigenia, must be killed. After much consternation, Agamemnon performed the deed before sailing for Troy, leaving behind an angry wife and family. This was only one of several follies awaiting the Greeks before the battle even began!

## Odysseus Feigns Madness

They needed cunning, so they sent for Odysseus, now the King of Ithaca. Odysseus had heard that Agamemnon was assembling a force to invade Troy and retrieve Helen for his brother, but he wanted neither conflict with Troy nor an enemy in Agamemnon. Again, relying on his wits, he began to feign madness.

The oath to honor the winner of the contest for Helen's hand in marriage was merely one of his tricks, so Odysseus did not feel bound by it. When Agamemnon's emissary, Palamedes, arrived, he found Odysseus dressed as a peasant, salting his crops and uttering absurdities. Unconvinced by what was admittedly *not his best ruse*, Palamedes placed the Ithacan king's son, Telemachus, in front of the plow Odysseus was using – a modern-day game of chicken – causing Odysseus to swerve and miss, betraying his own game. Proving himself sane and capable of saving his son, Odysseus was now bound to fight for Agamemnon or risk retaliation. Odysseus was tasked along with Nestor to continue rallying the Achaean kingdoms to their side, reminding them of the oath they had sworn to Menelaus at his betrothal to Helen. Diomedes, Ajax the Great, Ajax the Lesser, Idomeneus, and Menestheus all joined the cause, but they still needed the greatest warrior of all: Achilles.

### Achilles and Prophecy

Many years had now passed since the wedding of Thetis and Peleus, and they had given birth to a son they named Achilles. Though Zeus had forced Thetis to marry Peleus, she did not want a mortal son. Secretly, she visited the River Styx at the border of Hades, and once there, she dipped her infant son, holding him upside down by his heel. The river made Achilles invulnerable on all parts of his body submerged in the water, leaving only one point of weakness: the very heel his mother had held him by. Some versions of this myth have Peleus disagreeing with such treatment of his son, leading to the deaths of many of Achilles' would-be older siblings.

Like many characters in the Trojan War, Thetis had also been motivated to such dangerous lengths by a prophecy: that her son would be remembered forever as the world's greatest warrior, but that he would die as a young man. Thus, despite his seeming invulnerability, Thetis tried to hide Achilles from Agamemnon's envoys. Once he was found, she passed on the oracle's warning to Achilles. Now, Achilles would need to decide whether he would live long and be forgotten – or die young and be remembered. Due to arrogance that he could avoid such a fate or accept his heroic nature, he agreed to set sail with Agamemnon and the Greeks and lead his much-feared Myrmidon army against the Trojans.

### False Starts

Several years had passed in rousing the scattered and famously uncooperative Greek kingdoms, but the successful recruitment campaign led to an alliance of over one hundred thousand Achaean soldiers. This vast army would require over a thousand ships to ferry them across the sea to Anatolia and the beaches of Troy. They agreed to assemble at Aulis, where a series of follies began.

First, during their sacrifices to the gods to favor their side and maintain their goodwill, a snake slithered from beneath the alter, climbed a tree, ate eight sparrow chicks and their mother – and finally turned to stone. A seer named Calchas was present, who interpreted the strange omen to mean that the Achaean's war would last for *nine years* before they defeated the Trojans in the tenth. The soldiers took this omen with mixed emotions; yes, the war would end in victory for them, but it would last a grueling ten years. They set sail to Troy with hopeful but troubled minds and landed in Anatolia to unleash hell on the shores of the great city.

Unfortunately, the city they found was not Troy but rather Mysia, with Telephus, son of Heracles, as their king. Mysia was one of the Greek colonies in Anatolia, and a great and confusing battle ensued that ended with Telephus chasing the Achaeans off in a storm. Once again, they regrouped in Aulis.

The final folly came when Agamemnon, waiting in Aulis once again set sail to Troy, led a hunting party where he not only boasted that he was as great a hunter as the goddess Artemis but also unwittingly killed one of her sacred deer. In anger and vengeance, Artemis stopped all winds from blowing at Aulis, making it impossible for the Achaeans to depart for Troy. The oracle Calchas said that Artemis would only allow it to blow again once a blood sacrifice of Agamemnon's eldest daughter, Iphigenia, was made in return. Menelaus convinced him to send for her, telling her that she was to be married to the great Achilles.

Iphigenia and her mother, Clytemnestra, arrived only to learn it was a trap when they spoke to Achilles – who knew nothing of the plot. Furious at being made a pawn, Achilles told the armies why the winds had stopped and how Calchas had said they would blow again through the sacrifice of Iphigenia. Agamemnon had been close to changing his mind but was now caught between sacrificing his daughter and the murder of his whole family by the restless soldiers who were threatening to turn on him if he did not appease Artemis.

At this point, Iphigenia volunteered for the sacrifice, knowing that she would die either way and seeing an opportunity to save her mother and father. Because of her heroism, Artemis took pity on Iphigenia and spared her from the sacrifice, though her parents would not learn of her survival until later. With Artemis appeased, the winds returned, and the Achaeans set sail once again.

The Sacrifice of Iphigenia *by François Perrier. Credit: Wikimedia Commons*

They landed in one more place – still not Troy – and stayed long enough for Achilles to slay a son of Apollo. Also, one of the Achaean warriors came down with a mysterious, festering wound that would not heal.

The island they stopped at was called Tenedos, and they wished to resupply before arriving at Troy and commencing the war. The chief god of the island was Apollo, and King Tenes was his son. Achilles lusted after Tenes' sister, Hemithea, who escaped his advances, but the ordeal angered the king, ready to take arms against the great warrior. Thetis appeared and warned Achilles not to harm Tenes, as it would anger Apollo.

However, Achilles would not back down from the challenge, and the fight ended with Achilles driving his sword through the king's chest. As predicted by Thetis, Apollo swore revenge, sealing the fate of Achilles to die in the Trojan War. The Achaeans scrambled to make a sacrifice to appease Apollo, but again, a venomous snake slithered from the altar and bit Philoctetes of Meliboea on his foot. The wound would not heal and was so pungent that his confused and alarmed companions took him to the nearby island of Lemnos, where Philoctetes could heal until they returned for him. Now fully provisioned – but with a powerful enemy in Apollo –the Achaeans finished their journey to Troy.

# PART TWO: THE TROJAN WAR

# Chapter 5: The War Begins

Perhaps one of the reasons that the Achaeans were both eager to arrive yet seemingly dragging their feet was yet another prophecy by Calchas. She foretold that the first person to step foot on Trojan land would also be the first to die. Odysseus publicly dismissed the oracle's prediction while inwardly remaining cautious. Being pragmatic and knowing that someone had to start lest they rot on their ships, he leaped out of his boat but surreptitiously landed on his shield rather than Trojan soil, beginning the cascade of Achaean soldiers onto the beach.

The first to land firmly on the ground was Protesilaus, who promptly met his death at the hands of none other than Prince Hector – who was leading a charge outside of Troy's walls to greet the Achaeans while they were vulnerable and unfortified. The battle ended with the Achaean force depleted and the Trojans returning to safety behind their walls. The Greeks had won the beachhead at a high cost, though the Trojans were also bloodied; Achilles had fought and killed the famed and feared Cycnus, a son of Poseidon defending Troy.

## A Greek Envoy

Once the dust settled and the Achaean army was camped firmly within the Trojan territory, tradition called for one final attempt to avoid war. King Menelaus and King Odysseus were selected as the Greek envoy to negotiate for the return of Helen and the restoration of peace between the kingdoms. They were taken into the home of Antenor, a Trojan noble with many Greek connections both in family and in business. Menelaus would have his honor restored; Odysseus had simply been trying to avoid the gravity of the war since before his recruitment. Antenor gave a sympathetic ear to the Achaeans, each of whom would have been happy to return with Helen.

But peace was not truly in the cards, for King Priam was well and thoroughly trapped by this point. He had already welcomed Helen (and the treasure she came with) into his city, and to return her only after an army showed up would have been admitting he was wrong in the first place. His conundrum caught him between admission of wrongdoing or showing cowardice, or perhaps even *both*. The time to send Helen back to Sparta had long passed, and the meeting turned into nothing more than a formality.

What is more, Menelaus and Odysseus may not have known how close they came to their deaths. A Trojan named Antimachus lobbied for the murder of the kings, not only in retaliation for their invasion and bloodshed but to rob the Achaeans of two of its most important leaders. Menelaus was the symbolic cause of the war for the Trojans and Odysseus among the chief Achaean strategists. The Greeks would have been outraged by the murder plot, but likely would have questioned the logic of fighting to return Helen to a dead king. As a bonus, though they could not have known it at the time, the Trojans would have also eliminated the man that would deal them their death blow with the plot of the Trojan horse.

In the end, the two kings were escorted from the city as peacefully as they had been escorted into it, and both sides began preparing their next moves.

### A Long Stalemate

Calchas proved to be correct about the length of the war as it dragged on for nine long years. Troy was never fully under siege by the Greeks, despite the Achaeans controlling much of the Aegean shore and the Dardanelles. While they outnumbered the Trojan forces, they still lacked the numbers to completely encircle the city without spreading themselves too thin, becoming vulnerable to concentrated attacks. As a result, the Trojans maintained communication and trade with their allies and thus avoided the problems of starvation and plague that often come from locking a population inside of a citadel.

Breaching the citadel by brute force was another option for the Achaeans, but it was a bad option. Troy was not merely a city with a large wall around it but also a showcase in Bronze Age military technology. Around the outer wall was a wooden palisade and a trench dug eight to ten feet deep into the bedrock, nearly doubling its height and preventing any tunneling campaigns.

The palisade and trench also prevented their enemies from utilizing siege towers, so any attempt to crest the walls would have to be done with ladders or at the gates – which were defended far better. The citadel (fortification) found inside, called Pergamos, was even more impressive. Its thirty-foot walls sat atop a one-hundred-foot hilltop overlooking the surrounding plains. They were sixteen feet thick, mocking any attempts with a battering ram, and its defenders patrolled its 1100-foot perimeter behind parapets encircling the top. Every attempt by the Achaeans to break the defenses was repelled, with battle cries and then corpses filling the trenches.

Yet despite their elite defensive advantage, the Trojans were still far outnumbered and unable to capitalize after each repulsion of the enemy. Defending the mile-long perimeter of their outer walls required most of their forces and attention; sparing too many soldiers for open engagement would leave them exposed. Wary that the

Greeks might simply be attempting to lure them away from their defensive posts, the Trojans remained behind their walls.

However, Priam and Hector's strategy is often criticized for not including more ambushes and guerrilla campaigns against the Achaeans. These would have whittled down the invading warriors' numbers and devastated their morale, being so far from home and for so long. This strategy could have been implemented with forces small enough to avoid compromising their defense, and the absence of such attacks is what many non-Homeric sources use as evidence that the Trojans feared the Greeks.

Over time, the forces settled into a stalemate of sorts, with much of the fighting taking place away from the citadel where Troy's neighbors lacked such glorious walls. The Achaeans had no supply line to speak of, so they took over nearby cities and towns, becoming warlords in the countryside in order to farm and sustain themselves. Unsurprisingly, Achilles and Ajax the Greater were the two most active Achaean leaders in their raids. Achilles and his Myrmidons (mercenaries) laid claim to eleven Anatolian cities and twelve nearby islands.

Odysseus, for his part, busied himself with revenge against Palamedes, the man who recruited him for the war, spoiled his ruse, and endangered his infant son. Being discouraged by the length of the war, Palamedes began to encourage the leaders to give up and go home. The irony of it was too much for Odysseus, *who would not have even been there if not for Palamedes' insistence.* He seized the opportunity to frame Palamedes as a traitor by planting a fortune in Palamedes' tent and forging a letter from King Priam to be discovered along with the bribe. Odysseus claimed that Palamedeshe was working for Priam in trying to encourage retreat, resulting in a sentence of death by stoning – a punishment that Odysseus himself took part in. For all his cleverness, his pride was perhaps even larger. Had he merely sided with Palamedes, maybe he could have returned to Ithaca, Penelope, and their son. But he could not abide surrender, and he could not forgive Palamedes' wrongdoing. Besides, the tenth year of the war was approaching, and the oracle Calchas had not been wrong yet.

# Chapter 6: The Iliad

The *Iliad* is the "Story of Ilion," which was the Greek name for Troy. However, the events of Homer's *Iliad* all take place near the end of the war, and it centers around the rage of Achilles.

As you will see, revenge is core to the story. Achilles wants revenge on Agamemnon for taking away Briseus and for the death of his best friend, Patroclus (many today believe that the two were lovers, although the *Iliad* does not explicitly say this). This theme resounds throughout Homer's *Iliad* – and through many other ancient Greek poems and stories.

However, forgiveness is another theme, as Achilles' revenge does not bring him peace. Even making sacrifices to the gods (or dragging Hector's dead body by Chariot) does nothing to reduce his pain. Only by providing King Priam with twelve days of peace – enabling the King to mourn his son's death – does Achilles finally find a measure of peace. After all the battles and death, forgiveness is the key to unlocking his soul's reconciliation.

Aside from lessons of forgiveness, the *Iliad* can be viewed as history's first antiwar propaganda due to its perspective on battles and needless death. Its audience will often read of the horrors of war and the overall tragedy of the Trojan War. Descriptions include:

"He was standing on the stern of his deep-bellied ship, watching the grim toil of war and the miserable rout." *(Homer book 11, lines 600-601.*

"Daughter of Zeus the aegis-wearer, look at this! Shall we two give up caring about the Danaans as they die?" *(Homer book 8, lines 352-353)*

"They piled their dead on to a pyre in silence, grieving in their hearts...In the same way, the well-greaved Achaeans on their side piled their dead on to a pyre, grieving in their hearts" *(Homer book 7, lines 427-431)*

Aside from the lessons of war, Homer's book has garnered much historical significance – so much so that Alexander the Great slept with a copy of the *Iliad* every night! As one of the oldest pieces of literature around, this book is still taught in classrooms around the world today. Let us dive in.

The story picks up after Achilles and Agamemnon raided a nearby village and took two women as captives. Agamemnon claimed Chryseis, and Achilles took her sister, Briseis. The women's father, a man named Chryses (who served as a priest of the god Apollo), found Agamemnon and begged him to return his daughters. He offered to pay whatever ransom was required, yet Agamemnon refused.

Chryses did what most people did during those times; he sought the help of a god. He prayed to Apollo, who set loose a plague on the Achaeans camped outside of Troy. After ten days of watching his fellow Greeks drop dead, Achilles called upon Calchas to use his powers of prophecy to figure out what was going on. Calchas revealed that the plague was part of the vengeance of Apollo. As you will recall, Agamemnon had already found himself on the wrong side of Apollo more than once.

Having much arrogance, he could not succumb to complete defeat, so Agamemnon agreed to return Chryseis, but only if Achilles gave up Briseis as his compensation. As the leader of the Achaeans,

Agamemnon believed that he should have the greatest prize – and that he should be able to outwit adversaries.

Achilles, also always proud, was infuriated and threatened to leave Troy and return to Phthia if Agamemnon persisted. When Agamemnon threatened to charge into Achilles' tent to take Briseis on his own, it took the interference of Athena to prevent Achilles from drawing his sword on the Greek commander. Instead, Achilles backed down and let the King of Mycenae have what he wanted.

After returning to his tent, Achilles prayed to his mother, Thetis, to punish Agamemnon and the rest of the Achaeans for not backing him. Thetis agreed to take the matter to Zeus, who owed her a favor. At first, Zeus was reluctant to help since his wife Hera favored the Greeks. But seeing the opportunity to further reduce the potential demigod challengers to his throne, he agreed to honor the favor. Odysseus returned Chryseis to her father, who prayed to Apollo to lift the curse of pestilence spreading among the Achaeans. However, for many of them, their troubles were just beginning.

In a bold yet somewhat uncharacteristic move, Paris challenged any Achaean to single combat and was dismayed when Menelaus stepped forth. Paris lost his nerve and tried to back away through the Trojan ranks. This situation is somewhat surprising, as it is unclear who Paris thought would accept his challenge, and Menelaus was far from the most skilled warrior the Achaeans had to offer. Hector prevented the cowardly retreat by his brother, instead convincing Paris to duel Menelaus, the Spartan king. Paris found his courage again and declared that the winner would be Helen's rightful husband, an outcome that would effectively end the war.

As Paris and Menelaus were readying themselves for combat, Helen lay inside the city, completely unaware of the development. Per the story, Iris (Messenger of the Gods) disguised herself as Hector's sister and tipped Helen off about the fight, sending her to the city gates to watch. This was not to be the first – or last – time that gods intervened in this war.

The duel started with spears and then moved to swords, and Menelaus gained the upper hand when he cracked Paris over the head with his sword and began dragging him around by his helmet. Aphrodite (goddess of love, beauty, pleasure, passion, and procreation), still siding with the Trojans for Paris' judgment, unfastened the helmet's strap so that Paris could break free of the Spartan's grip. This interference only garnered a brief moment for Paris. As Menelaus was sending a fatal blow of his spear to his opponent's chest, Aphrodite interfered again, instantly transporting Paris back to his room in the palace.

Helen found him there, scolded him, and then laid down with him.

There was great confusion outside of the gates, as the Prince of Troy seemed to have magically vanished rather than being run through by the spear! Agamemnon declared Menelaus the victor and demanded the return of Helen. Of course, Paris and Helen refused, and the Trojan royals backed them.

With the hope of ending the war through single combat vanished, the war raged on. Diomedes and the Trojan hero, Pandarus, met on the battlefield, and Diomedes was badly wounded. Diomedes was one of Goddess Athena's favorite warriors, so she healed him and gave him godlike strength. She also gave him the power to see the gods and goddesses on the field of battle, whose actions had been hidden to him and remained hidden to the other soldiers. She told him that he was not to challenge or harm any of the gods, save Aphrodite.

With his new abilities, he once again found Pandarus on the battlefield, whom he skewered brutally on his spear. He also seriously wounded Aeneas and cut his mother's wrist, Aphrodite, when she went to help him. While Athena's rules permitted this, he went too far when Apollo came to the aid of Aeneas and was attacked by Diomedes as well.

With ease, Apollo pushed Diomedes aside and removed Aeneas from the battlefield to be healed. To punish Diomedes, Apollo left the image of Aeneas' body on the ground to rouse anger among the

Trojans – and brought Ares (the Greek god of war) to fight by their side.

All the divine intervention led to the Trojans gaining the upper hand, with Hector and Ares forming a fierce tandem. Hera and Athena became fearful that the tide was turning against them and convinced Zeus to allow them to help the Achaeans.

Ever playing both sides, Zeus agreed.

Athena told Diomedes that he could fight anyone he wanted, and he managed to wound Ares by charging him with a chariot, transporting him back to Mt. Olympus and out of the battle. Athena and Hera decided it was safe to leave after Ares had been dispatched, as the Achaeans were the superior force *when no gods were getting in the way*.

To end the day's ferocious battle and prevent a further advance by the Greeks, Hector emerged to challenge any Achaean to single combat. Menelaus was again the first to step forward, but Agamemnon convinced him that while he easily handled the last prince, he was no match for this one. Nine other Achaeans stepped forward and commenced having a lottery among them; Ajax the Great was chosen as the Achaean champion. Ajax had been described as more of a wall than a man, and Hector knew immediately that he had his work cut out for him. After fighting with spears and lances with no apparent victor, they were about to draw swords when Zeus intervened to call off the fight due to nightfall.

A pact of friendship was made between the warriors, and Hector managed to prevent the Greek forces from taking more Trojan lives. Still, corpses littered the fields, and both sides agreed on a day's truce to tend to their dead.

During the truce, Zeus also forbade the gods from re-entering the war until he decided which side he would favor. At Mt. Ida in Anatolia, he placed the fates of the Achaeans and Trojans in his scales and sided with Troy when the Greek side plunked down.

In a great storm of lightning, Zeus struck out at the Achaean encampment, all of which began to flee in fear. Hector and the Trojans took advantage of the chaos, sensing a turning point and seeing an opportunity to rid themselves of the Achaeans on their shore. They cut down the retreating Greeks who were starting to make for their ships, and as Hera and Athena were about to help them, Zeus warned them again not to intervene. One would hope this would be the end of battling, but pride took the forefront once again. The Achaeans convinced Zeus to give them one more chance, to which he replied that only Achilles could save them.

Meanwhile, night had fallen on the Achaean retreat, and Hector ordered that campfires be lit so that they could not escape in the dark. The Achaeans sat in despair, with Agamemnon weeping at the thought of returning to Greece in disgrace. Diomedes declared that he would continue fighting even if he were the only one left standing; the Achaeans began to take heart once more in the prophecy of Calchas that declared they were destined to win.

Nestor recommended that Agamemnon make amends with Achilles so that he would return and fight with them once more – and Agamemnon agreed. He sent Odysseus and Ajax the Great a great heap of wealth and fortune on the condition that they returned to the war.

Once back at the battlefield, they found Achilles in his tent, relaxed and playing the lyre with his long-time friend and deputy Patroclus. The two had grown up together and shared a bond so close that scholars are left unsure of whether they may have also been lovers, something fairly common among Achaean soldiers. Upon hearing the offer, Achilles rejected it outright, reciting his plans to return home to Phthia; the Achaean forces returned to their despair.

Hector and Ajax the Great met once again in battle, and once again, they fought to a draw. The Trojans kept pushing them back until – as the story goes – Hector was close enough to touch a ship. Upon seeing this, Patroclus gives in, telling Achilles that he will go and join the fight in an effort to save the ships. As Achilles still refused to join in the battle, Patroclus asked if he could wear his armor; Achilles agreed. Patroclus and the Myrmidons rushed to help push back the Trojan advance, and Achilles prayed for the safety of both the ships and of Patroclus. Homer tells us that Zeus would only grant *one* of those prayers.

At the sight of Achilles' armor, the Trojans (or those who were *able to*) immediately retreated from the Achaean ships. Many had their retreat cut short by the sudden and unexpected entrance of new combatants; Patroclus dispatched them with great prejudice, including Zeus' mortal son Sarpedon. While Zeus accepted his son's death without intervention, he decided that Patroclus had to die in return. Seeing so many retreating Trojans, Patroclus broke his word to Achilles by pursuing Hector's forces.

At the gates of the city, Hector turned to meet the foe that he still believed to be Achilles, and the two engaged in single combat. During the fight, Hector realized that his foe was not actually Achilles; and so he slew Patroclus, taunting with the words:

*"Wretch! Achilles, great as he was, could do nothing to help you."*

Patroclus' last words to Hector foretold his enemy's pending doom:

*"You yourself are not one who shall live long, but now already death and powerful destiny are standing beside you, to go down under the hands of Peleus' great son, Achilles."*

In the immediate aftermath, Trojans and Greeks began to fight over Achilles' armor, but Hector snatches the armor, taking it back to the city.

When Achilles heard of Patroclus's death, he began a violent breakdown. His anguished wails were loud enough that Thetis heard and came to see what troubled him. Knowing that she could no longer sway him against the life of a warrior, she begged him to wait one day before seeking vengeance. This, she argued, would allow time for

Hephaestus (Greek god of blacksmiths, metalworking, carpenters, craftsmen, artisans, etc.) to make him a new set of armor, replacing the one taken by Hector.

Each army began constructing new plans and strategies now that Achilles was returning to the battle. The Trojans considered returning to the safety of their walls, but Hector refused, not wanting to cede any of the ground they had gained over the recent weeks.

Thetis returned the next day to give Achilles his new body armor, promising to look after Patroclus' body. Donning his new armor and attending the Achaean assembly, Achilles formally reconciled with Agamemnon, who made good on his promise of gifts – and Briseus – in exchange for him resuming the battle. Achilles vowed to do nothing, *not even eat*, until Hector was dead by his hand. Achilles' seething wrath was so great that Zeus feared that he might tear down the entire Trojan civilization before it was time. The rest of the gods had no longer wanted to interfere but rather took up seats to watch how the end would play out with the mortals on their own – and Achilles in a far more murderous temper than usual.

Achilles charged the Trojans near the Scamander River, killing so many of them that the river became clogged and dammed with bodies. The river gods were overwhelmed by what was happening and called on the gods of Mt. Olympus for help. Hearing the plea, Achilles was attacked by the river and dragged downstream until the Hephaestus (the god of blacksmiths) boiled the water out of the river until it released Achilles. During this melee, most of the gods and goddesses watching the unfolding events had whipped themselves into such a frenzy that they began fighting each other.

Meanwhile, King Priam opened the gates of Troy to allow his soldiers to retreat and escape Achilles' pursuit and was barely able to shut them in time before Achilles could enter from behind. Hector, alone, remained outside of the gates, ashamed of his decision not to retreat – a decision that had gotten so many Trojans killed. Zeus once again went to Mt. Ida to judge fates, this time that of Achilles and

Hector, now facing each other for the first time in the war. Placing their futures on the scales, Hector's side fell with a clank, bringing Patroclus' final words closer to fruition.

Alone and outside the walls of Troy, the two great warriors clashed spears once again. Knowing Hector's armor, Achilles was able to quickly exploit a weakness in the neck when Hector charged him. Fallen and struggling through his wound, Hector asks that Achilles gives him a proper burial, but the Achaean was still in a mind of vengeance and told him that his body would be for the birds and dogs before driving his spear through the Trojan prince's chest. Watching from atop the city walls, Priam, Hecuba, and Andromache looked helplessly on as Achilles tied Hector's body to the back of his chariot and dragged him around the city. For days, Achilles continued to desecrate the corpse of Hector as he mourned Patroclus. Finally, King Priam himself left the walls of Troy with the help of Hermes and slipped into Achilles' tent to offer him a ransom for his son's body. He connected with Achilles' better side when he asked him to think of the love between fathers and sons and the love he holds for his father, Peleus. Achilles accepted the ransom, and Priam left to care for his son's body.

*A fresco depicting the scene of Achilles's triumph. This was painted by Franz Matsch. Credit: Wikimedia Commons.*

# Chapter 7: The Deaths of Penthesilea, Memnon, and Achilles

While the *Iliad* ended with Hector's funeral, the Trojan War continued. Troy had lost its native hero with the prince's death, but they were about to get some help from an impressive ally: the Amazons.

### Who were the Amazons?

According to Greek mythology, the Amazons were a race of warrior women who were frequently pitted against the Greeks. Their territory was somewhere around the Black Sea, and many scholars place their homeland as far north as Ukraine. A queen led these warriors, and in order to keep their society going, they would find mates – but only kept the female children. The girls would grow up to become warriors like their mothers, and the boys would be abandoned, killed, or given up depending upon the telling of the story.

*A depiction of an Amazon. Credit: Wikimedia Commons.*

The name "Amazon" has associations with South America today, but the Greek roots are "a-mazos," which means "without breast." That is one theory that gave rise to stories claiming that the warriors would cut off their right breast so that it could not interfere with their archery or spear thrusts. Still, artistic depictions of the Amazons show them with both breasts, leading many to believe that the Greek name for them is metaphorical, as they had shunned what the Greeks would have considered being a woman's life for that of a man's by virtue of becoming warriors. The final explanation is simpler: the Greek name probably comes from the name they called themselves, which has roots in another language less understood and further lost than Ancient Greek.

Archaeological evidence gives some further insight into the debate as to whether this group existed or were figments of the collective Greek psyche. Using DNA testing on remains in Scythian graves, archaeologists discovered that many of the bodies once thought to be men were Scythian women. What led to this misconception?

The women had been buried with their weapons and with wounds and scarring consistent with those of warriors. In other words, archaeologists found bodies decorated as warriors and assumed for centuries that they were, therefore, *men*. Plenty of the graves were indeed for men, but the egalitarian internment shows that Scythian women were just as likely to train for war.

Further, the Scythian territory is consistent with the regions described as *Amazon territory* by the Greeks. Scythians were also a horse culture credited with the innovation of a saddle, both things that would have further leveled the playing field of war by removing many of the size and strength retorts that are common – even today – when discussing female soldiers. Coming this far, it is not ridiculous to assume that there was egalitarian leadership as well or even (*gasp*) a matriarchy in power during this period.

A matriarchy would support the practice of choosing to raise the girls and sending the boys to be raised by their fathers, not killing them. Their portrayal as man-haters is also undone, even by the Greeks themselves. They are described as man-killers, naturally, since that is primarily who they would have been fighting against. Being further described as fierce warriors, they would have been very good at it. But they were also highly sexualized in Ancient Greek stories, as can be seen in the Labors of Heracles.

### The Amazons and the Ninth Labor of Heracles

Pre-dating their entry into the Trojan War, the Amazons were part of the story of Heracles' twelve labors. (In case you are wondering, the story is also called the Labors of Hercules; in one version, Hercules is a god. In this version, Heracles is a mere mortal.)

His ninth labor was to retrieve the belt of Hippolyte, the Queen of the Amazons at the time. According to the story, he arrives and informs her of his quest, to which she consents. However, Hera was dismayed at the ease with which he was about to accomplish his task and disguised herself as one of the Amazons to engage in a misinformation campaign. She told her fellow warriors that the Greeks had come not for the belt but *war* and that they would soon be killed if they did not stand and fight. As Heracles was about to receive the belt from Hippolyte, his soldiers were attacked by the Amazon forces, and he drew his sword and killed their queen, removing her belt once she was dead.

That is one way of telling the story, but it does not make much sense at face value. Why did Hera task Heracles with getting a queen's belt? As usual, symbolism matters here. In Ancient Greek culture, obtaining (or *taking*) a woman's belt represented a sexual conquest, especially of a virgin. What Hera truly required Heracles to do was either seduce or rape the Queen of the Amazons. Read this way, Heracles was initially successful in courting Hippolyte, which was a great surprise to Hera. With Hera's next actions remaining the same, the metaphor tells us that Heracles killed and then raped Hippolyte, symbolized by taking the belt off her body *afterward*. Our hero.

### Achilles versus Queen Penthesilea

There is another version of the myth where Heracles abducts rather than kills Hippolyte after taking her "belt" and returns to Athens with Theseus, who then marries the queen. In retribution for this abduction, the Amazons, led by Hippolyte's sister Penthesilea, attack Athens to rescue her. Or they attacked Athens after Theseus discarded the Amazon queen in favor of Phaedra, the daughter of King Minos of Crete. Hippolyte, who either still loved or irreconcilably hated Theseus, was accidentally killed by Penthesilea. (Or none of that happened, and Hippolyte was killed by her sister with a spear during a deer-hunting accident.) The Ancient Greeks sometimes had difficulty keeping their stories straight. Regardless of the fate of Hippolyte, Penthesilea was Queen of the Amazons at the time of the Trojan War, and she sided with the Trojans like her father Ares had.

The Achaeans were devastated by her arrival, and she cut through their forces with more tenacity than even the recently dispatched Prince Hector had. Once again, it was up to Achilles to prove his status as the greatest warrior of the conflict and challenge the queen to single combat. The Greek storytellers once again have a hard time agreeing on what happened next. In some rarer but still prevalent versions, Penthesilea shocks everyone, including the gods, by slaying the mighty Achilles. Zeus decided that this could not be the end for the hero, so Achilles was resurrected and promptly killed Penthesilea. There was no mercy resurrection for the fallen queen, and everyone was allowed to overlook such an embarrassing almost-moment. Most versions, however, are more straightforward and tell of Achilles slaying Penthesilea fair-and-square and then falling in love with her when he removes her helmet and sees her face.

### Achilles versus Memnon

Yet another challenger to Achilles was Memnon, King of Ethiopia. As a nephew of Priam, Memnon decided to come to the Trojans' aid late in the war, bringing with him a strong army and providing renewed hope for Troy. Memnon himself was the son of the Titan Eos and was described in the echelon of Achilles, Hector, Ajax the Great, and Penthesilea as a warrior. In a battle where the Trojans had begun to route the Achaean forces, Prince Paris shot and wounded the horse pulling the chariot of the aged King Nestor of Pylos.

With Nestor stuck, his son Antilochus came to his aid and engaged Memnon, whose army was pursuing the retreating Greeks. Memnon killed Antilochus, and afterward, a grief-stricken Nestor challenged Memnon to single combat. Seeing that Nestor was too old for it to be a fair fight, Memnon refused. Nestor then approached Achilles with the task, appealing to his pride by claiming that there was another warrior many believed to be his equal.

Thetis appeared, pleading with her son to turn down this fight since a vision of hers told her that Achilles would die soon after the death of Memnon. But believing that this would prove once and for all that he was the mightiest hero, Achilles accepted and confronted Memnon outside the gates of Troy. During the fight, Memnon wounded Achilles in his arm, marking the first time blood was drawn against the seemingly invincible demigod. Still, while Memnon was able to match Achilles in strength, the Achaean's speed was too much, and Memnon fell with a spear through his heart.

*Combat between Achilles and Memnon. Credit: Ron Koopman, Wikimedia Commons.*

### Death of Achilles

If there is one thing to take away from the story of the Trojan War, it is that prophecies will be fulfilled. People could fight them or accept them, but they came true all the same. Heroes and even the gods themselves lived by them and often died by them.

Achilles had been told on many occasions that he would die if he fought in the Trojan War. It was on his mother's mind when he departed the island of Skyros to prove his valor. It was on the lips of the fallen Hector as Achilles stood gloating over the prince's dimming eyes. When prophecy finally came to claim Achilles, though, it came from an unlikely source. While he may have lived a warrior's life and compiled an impressive resume of kills, he died ingloriously when Prince Paris shot him from afar with a poison-tipped arrow and with the spiteful guidance of the Apollo. The combination of ambush, poison, and divine intervention leaves Paris with little credit for killing Achilles, and even in victory, he is remembered as cowardly.

In some versions, it is not even Paris, but Apollo *disguised as Paris,* who delivers the fatal shot, completely removing him from the event. Either way, portraying the downfall of Achilles in this manner allowed for the realization of the seemingly contradictory prophecy that he would be the greatest warrior (and therefore undefeated in battle) and yet still die in the war.

*Achilles as he lay dying. Credit: Wikimedia Commons.*

In the 1995 article titled "Achilles' Heel: The Death of Achilles in Ancient Myth," Jonathon Burgess cites evidence from ancient art and literature, arguing that Achilles was most likely killed outside the walls of Troy with two arrows. The first arrow landed on his ankle, disabling him and stripping him of his legendary speed. The second one is said to have killed him. Indeed, in the later Roman myth, he was shot in the heel while inside Apollo's temple.

The question of Achilles' manner of death is simple; the answer is complex. But that is part and parcel of mythology – it is seldom straightforward. Achilles is a fictional character (we think), so one can choose whichever story most appeals to him.

# Chapter 8: Ajax's Death and the Last Prophecies

Following the death of Achilles, Ajax the Great and Odysseus fought off a horde of Trojans to retrieve the body of the fallen warrior. Ajax heaved Achilles, his armor, and his weapons atop of the brick wall that was his shoulders, and Odysseus fought ferociously to hold the opposing soldiers at bay. Achilles' armor had been forged on Mt. Olympus by the god Hephaestus, and both Ajax and Odysseus coveted it for its craftsmanship and magical protective properties.

While their intentions in hauling Achilles back to the Achaean camp may have been pure, they quickly devolved into a squabble over who deserved their comrade's armor more. Having been the one to do the literal heavy lifting, Ajax claimed that he played the more essential role – especially since Odysseus could not have managed the dead warrior's weight. Conversely, Odysseus pointed out that Ajax would have joined him as a corpse had he not been there to fight off the rabid Trojans.

Both, of course, were right.

To settle the dispute, they argued before a council of high-ranking Achaeans. The contest was, of course, over before it began, with Ajax agreeing to a battle of wits with Odysseus amid a Greek myth. Athena aided Odysseus to make his speech more eloquent and to enchant the ears of the council. The armor was eventually awarded to Odysseus, and, in grief, Ajax plunged his own sword into his chest.

This suicidal response is as famous in Greek mythology as it is confusing. The image of Ajax falling on his sword is a popular image found on Greek pottery and seemed embedded in the ancient civilization's culture. Still, the reaction seems out of proportion to what had occurred. Odysseus even finds Ajax in the underworld during his journeys, and the great warrior is still angry with him over the armor dispute! The takeaway by most scholars is that this part of the tale shows how seriously the Achaeans took their honor.

Ajax had twice fought Hector to a duel and was widely regarded as nearly as invulnerable as Achilles himself. The soldier who wore the armor was symbolically the greatest Achaean warrior, an honor which Ajax was correct in expecting to fall to him. The fact that it goes to Odysseus was a grave dishonor to Ajax but perhaps marks a turning point in the story.

Odysseus was obviously inferior to Ajax in a fair fight, but Odysseus hated fair fights and was clever enough to avoid them. Similarly, the Achaeans brought more and better warriors with them than those who were defending Troy, but after a decade, they were still camped outside of its walls. It was no longer speed, strength, and honor in battle through which the Achaeans would win – but through strategy and ruthlessness. Thus, Odysseus was the best warrior for victory in the times to come, while Ajax was merely the superior fighter in the heretofore losing effort.

Nearly on cue, Odysseus captured Helenus, a Trojan prince who had left the city for Mt. Ida following a dispute with his family and forced him to give them intelligence. Helenus was a seer as well as a warrior, something that he had used on several occasions to defeat the Achaeans on the battlefield. Now, he was forced under torture to use his ability to tell his captors how they could breach the city walls and win the war.

He told them that to do so, they must recruit Achilles's son, Neoptolemus, and that they must retrieve Philoctetes (a famous archer from Lemnos, who had survived his abandonment and was in possession of Heracles legendary bow and poisonous arrows).

*A depiction of Philoctetes on Lemnos. Note Heracles's bow sitting beside him. Credit: Marie-Lan Nguyen, Wikimedia Commons.*

Recruiting the son of Achilles proved the simpler of the two, as Philoctetes and his Achaean compatriots had not parted ways on the best of terms. After receiving a mysterious, oozing wound on his foot that would not heal, his fellow warriors had simply left him behind so they could get on with their war. They feared taking him with them, not knowing if his weeping limb could somehow infect them as well.

So, he was left alone. His Bronze Age quarantine ended when prophecy dictated that he was needed. Odysseus and Diomedes headed the mission to retrieve him and were astonished to find him both still alive and still wounded. Odysseus had been the loudest voice in advocating to leave Philoctetes, a fact that both warriors were well aware of at their reunion, with Philoctetes clutching Heracles' poisonous arrows. Odysseus managed to trick Philoctetes into handing over the bow and arrow, but Diomedes stood firm and refused to leave with only the weapons and not their old friend.

Heracles himself, now a god, had to intervene to break the stalemate. He promised that if he agreed to go, Philoctetes would be healed by the son of the god Asclepius, thus becoming a great hero in the conclusion of the war for the Achaean army. He also dictated that it must be Philoctetes the wielded his former weapon. In a sign of good things to come for the Greeks, Philoctetes immediately showed his worth by using his poison arrows to kill Prince Paris, hitting him three times before landing the fourth arrow in his heel, just as he (and Apollo) had done to Achilles.

With two new recruits on hand, the Achaeans were halfway towards realizing the demands of Helenus' prophecy.

The third condition for a Greek victory was stealing the Palladium of Troy from within its walls. The Palladium was a sacred wooden statue of Athena (*Pallas* to the Trojans) that fell from the sky during the founding of Troy; the statue had since been worshipped as a protective talisman of the city. Again, Odysseus and Diomedes teamed up for the task, being the two best scalpels in an age of swords and spears.

Here, it is important to remember that Troy was not completely under siege and that people were able to come and go through certain city gates, heavily guarded as they might be. In some accounts of the story, Odysseus was able to gain entry disguised as a beggar and later let Diomedes in through a secret entrance he opened from the inside.

In other stories, they were aided by an ally inside the city, likely Antenor, who had mediated between the Achaeans and the Trojans at the onset of the war. Once inside, the two Achaeans did some sneaking and a little bit of killing before being recognized by Helen. Ever the double agent and skilled in her own survival, Helen decided to show the Achaeans where to find the Palladium. They left the city in the same way they had entered; the third condition for the prophecy to Troy had been met.

However, a larger question is posed by these events. If they were able to enter the city to steal the Palladium, then what need was there for the theatrics and, frankly, the unnecessary risks of the Trojan Horse?

There is no end to sussing out history from the metaphor and entertainment inherent in Greek myths, and this is one of the more interesting points to linger on. One possible answer is that the theft of the Palladium was not a literal theft. If the Palladium was a symbol for the protection of Troy, then perhaps this story is about the symbolic theft of the safety the walls afforded them when the Greeks found (or were aided in finding) a way into the city. Troy falling after the Greeks had an entry point through their walls makes a lot more sense, at least to modern readers, than Troy falling because they lost a statue.

The final task of Helenus' prophecy was to bring the bones of Pelops to Troy. Pelops was the grandfather of Agamemnon, who was buried in Pisa, so the Mycenaean king immediately dispatched a ship and crew tasked with digging up his relative and bringing back his remains.

However, as they returned, the ship was lost in a storm, and the bones never made it to Troy. This is another odd development, as it prevents the Achaeans from fulfilling the prophecy. Anyone who has been paying attention knows that prophecies were *law to* the Achaean Greeks, and the Greeks were still able to win despite their failure. Additionally, why include it in the prophecy if they do not achieve it? Do prophecies matter, or not? Unlike the story of the Palladium (seemingly creating a fantastic tale that confounds the reader), this one needs a fantastic tale *to help it make sense.*

Let us start from the beginning. The story of Pelops opens with his murder. His father, Tantalus, killed his son as part of his plan to test whether the gods were actually omniscient.

Tantalus cut Pelops into pieces, serving him in a stew offered to the god. Most of the gods knew something was amiss with the meal and refused to eat. Demeter, however, she ate Pelops' left shoulder. Later, the gods reassembled Pelops, brought him back to life, while the blacksmith god Hephaestus created an ivory shoulder to replace the one eaten by Demeter.

Hold on; it gets better.

Poseidon then made Pelops his apprentice in Olympus, teaching him how to steer the divine chariot. After going to Greece, Pelops entered a chariot race against Pisa's king Oenomaus – who feared a prophesy that he would be killed by his son-in-law. Oenomaus killed all his daughter's potential suitors – who were his challengers in the chariot races - to thwart the prophecy.

Pelops, hearing of this, asked for Poseidon's help. They convinced the king's charioteer to replace the bolts of his chariot wheels with fake ones. It worked. Oenomaus' chariot was destroyed during the race, and Oenomaus was dragged to death by his horses. Pelops was declared the winner, made king of Pisa, and married Oenomaus's daughter.

Back to one of Heracles labors . . . many believe, therefore, it was not his *bones,* but his *bone* that was required to be brought to Troy. This story makes much more sense, as there would be nothing special about the dead king's bones except for *the one that a goddess created.*

Specifically, Demeter – the one who ate Pelops in her stew – was the goddess of the harvest and had remained neutral through the war, unlike her more excitable brothers and sisters. Demeter's support would have likely come in the form of a good harvest for the

Achaeans in a time of need, or by depriving the besieged Trojans of a harvest. The ivory bone was a gift from Demeter, so perhaps this was what they needed; not the brittle remains of a long-dead king, but generosity from the goddess of the harvest.

Bottom line: the fates either said that three out of four was not bad, or they counted the fourth task symbolically, and the Greeks hatched their final scheme to take the city.

# Chapter 9: The Trojan Horse and the Sack of Troy

There is almost universal agreement that the city of Troy existed, though debate might still rage regarding its scale and whether Homer was prone to embellishments in his poetic descriptions. Likewise, the war between the Achaean Greeks and the Trojans is thought to have occurred even if there is ongoing deliberation in academia about its length and significance.

The Trojan Horse, on the other hand, is almost entirely dismissed by scholars as a complete invention.

Still, it is as iconic as a symbol for the fall of the Trojans as it is a testament to the Achaean's victory, and the tale cannot be concluded without it. Through scheming, it accomplished what even Achilles could not do through brawn when it finally allowed the Greeks to breach the walls of Troy.

*A depiction of the Trojan Horse by Giovanni Domenico Tiepolo. Credit: Wikimedia Commons.*

### The Legend of the Trojan Horse

According to the legend, Odysseus devised the scheme to build a giant, hollow wooden horse that an elite force of Achaean soldiers could hide inside of. The trick would be getting the Trojans to bring this horse into the city, so the first thing they had to do was convince the Trojans that they had left. To do this, they departed in the night for the island of Tenedos, where their fleet could remain nearby but not a present threat to Troy. The horse, therefore, was to remain as a gift to the Trojans, whom the Achaeans were declaring the victors.

The Trojans sent a party to investigate the newly deserted beach and the large wooden structure left where – for a decade – the Greek armies had camped. Among those sent to scrutinize the unexpected trophy was a priest named Laocoon. He famously claimed, upon reaching the horse, "I don't trust the Greeks even bearing gifts." He suggested that they light the equine sculpture on fire and be done with it, but Athena intervened by sending serpents that leaped out of the sea and killed Laocoon and his two sons that had accompanied him. Fearing now that refusing or burning the gift would anger the gods, the

Trojans decided to bring the wooden horse through the gates and throw a commemorative feast in honor of the gods and their victory. Cassandra, cursed with prophecies that no one would believe, also advised her father, Priam, against bringing the gift inside the walls, declaring that the Achaeans would destroy them if they did so. Her advice was not heeded, and the wooden horse remained an object of celebration as the Trojans ate and drank deep into the night.

Meanwhile, Odysseus, Diomedes, Menelaus, Philoctetes, Ajax the Lesser, and about twenty other Achaeans were inside the horse. They waited in a dreadful, cramped silence for days as the Trojans debated between burning them alive, pulling them through the gates, or leaving them to starve on the beach. Eventually, they brought them into the city and threw a feast in honor of the gods and their victory. As dawn approached, the streets finally quieted, and they were alone. Odysseus and his gang had little trouble fighting their way to the gates through the surprised and largely inebriated Trojans. There, the Achaean army met them after having returned unseen in the night. A fire signal had tipped them off that it was time to return and had stealthily anchored their boats outside the city once more. After ten years, the Trojans had let their guard down for one night, and the storming Achaeans saw to it that their mistake was fatal.

### A Contemporary Explanation

That is the typical story, with slightly different versions obligatorily splintering towards infinity. Historians and archaeologists take issue with it because it does not quite mesh with what they know of warfare in the region in the late Bronze Age. That is not to say that the Greeks would have been incapable of building the horse but rather that it was not a very good trick; an opponent such as the Trojans would have been well-aware of structures built to hide soldiers and breach walls. From the perspective of the Achaeans, the plan carried an incredibly high risk of failure and horrific death for those attempting to smuggle themselves.

It is worth noting, however, that Homer, Greek dramatists, and Greek historians have had a surprisingly impressive track record of archaeological evidence corroborating their claims, so perhaps it is wise not to discount the horse legend completely. If the gift were to have been used as a decoy rather than transportation, most of the story would still hold together. After all, Odysseus had already managed to sneak into the city on several occasions. Perhaps he could have done so again with a few of his friends while King Priam and the Trojan forces were thoroughly preoccupied with the elaborate and suspicious gift left on the beach. Regardless, what is generally agreed upon is that after a protracted war (lasting up a decade), the besieged Trojans were tricked into lowering their defenses, and the Achaeans made them pay.

## The Sack of Troy

The tables had turned. The same walls that had kept the Achaeans out and the Trojan citizens safe for many years were now trapping them inside for slaughter. In accordance with warfare of the time, the sack of Troy was brutal. The Achaeans, fueled by a decade of frustration and defeat, slaughtered Trojan men, women, and children in their sleep. Those who were not killed were raped or abducted – and often both. The Trojan soldiers, though surprised, were certain to have put up a fierce fight through the night and into the next day, but they were never able to recover. The Achaeans were also happy to let fire do what their swords and spears could not. Fire was their ally, as it brought Trojan warriors out of ambush and the Trojan structures to the ground. To escape the fires, many affluent Trojans suddenly became propertyless refugees. In the ruins of Troy, precious metal jewelry has been found in people's homes, indicative of their rapid and thoughtless flight for their lives.

As bad as the fall of Troy was for ordinary Trojans, it was perhaps worse for the Trojan royalty, who were singled out for destruction and vengeance. King Priam was found by Neoptolemus, the son of Achilles, at the altar of Zeus, where he was executed without pomp.

Odysseus, fearing that the same cycle of violence could one day repeat upon the Achaeans, found Hector's child son, Astyanax, and threw him to his death from atop the city walls. Hector's wife Andromache was taken by Neoptolemus and his sister Cassandra by Agamemnon. Each returned with the Achaeans to Greece to live as concubines to the warriors. Princess Polyxena, who some stories say was betrothed to Achilles before his death – was sacrificed on the demigod's grave. Helen, for whom the war was begun, awaited King Menelaus in her chambers. After the death of Paris, Helen had married one of his brothers, Deiphobus, whom Menelaus had slain moments earlier during the sack of the city. However, upon seeing her, he was overcome by her beauty and dropped his sword, and the two went back to Sparta as king and queen.

The Burning of Troy *by Johann Georg Trautmann.* Credit: Wikimedia Commons.

### The Flight of Aeneas

Among the refugees of Troy was Aeneas, the son of a Trojan prince, Anchises, and the goddess, Aphrodite. Until the age of five, Aeneas was raised by nymphs on Mt. Ida before being returned to his father, who had sworn never to tell that he had lain with a goddess. He was widely regarded as one of the best Trojan warriors in the war, though he was not as mighty as the likes of Hector or in the ranks of Achilles, Ajax, or Diomedes on the Achaean side. A better comparison may be Odysseus, though perhaps a little less cunning and a little more honorable.

Like Odysseus, Aeneas was favored by the gods, who twice rescued him from battle when it seemed that death was inevitable. Also, like Odysseus, Aeneas would face a long and arduous trip after the Trojan War. With his home destroyed, he fled the city with his son, father, and many other companions after receiving instructions to do so from the gods, who did not want to see the legacy of Troy completely forgotten.

Aeneas Flees Burning Troy *by Federico Barocci. Credit: Wikimedia Commons.*

Aeneas and his crew were tasked with founding a new city that would eventually birth another great civilization: Rome. Predictably, much of this story is fleshed out by a Roman poet rather than a Greek one, centuries after Homer wrote his *Iliad* and *Odyssey* tales. The Roman poet was named Virgil, and in the *Aeneid*, he told of the meandering adventure that Aeneas and his crew undertook. Their travels took them all around the Mediterranean, with notable stops in Crete, Sicily, and Carthage, where he met and fell in love with Queen Dido. Aeneas had to be reminded by the gods of his mission, and after he secretly absconded from Carthage, a heartbroken Dido uttered a prophecy and curse that would pit their descendants in Carthage and Rome against one another in the Punic Wars (before killing herself upon a sword left to her by Aeneas).

When Aeneas arrived in Italy, he was initially welcomed by Latinus, king of the Latins. However, all did not remain well when Latinus received a prophecy that his daughter, Lavinia, would marry a man from another land. Interpreting this as Aeneas, Latinus heeded the prophecy, which enraged neighboring King Turnus of the Rutuli. Allied with the Etruscans, Turnus marched to war against the Latins and their new Trojan allies. Aeneas himself killed Turnus to win the final battle, but Latinus was killed in the war.

Aeneas founded the city Lavinium, named after his wife, and stayed there with his people for the remainder of his life. When he died, Aphrodite negotiated with Zeus to grant him immortality. He was cleansed by the river god Numicus and given nectar and ambrosia by his mother so that he could ascend to the pantheon. Many generations later, his legendary descendants Romulus and Remus would found the city of Rome, but it is Aeneas and Lavinia who are seen as the progenitors of the Roman people.

When looked at anthropologically, this story makes a lot of sense. As a story written by Romans, it connected them to antiquity and gave their leaders more legitimacy in the eyes of their subjects. The alliance with the Latins and the conflicts with the Rutuli, Etruscans, and

Carthaginians all serve to explain the historical relationships between the people of the region. The relationship between Rome and Carthage that led to the Punic Wars mirrors that of the rivalry between the Greeks and Trojans before them. Roman historians even write admiringly of the Carthaginian general Hannibal, much the way that the Greeks honored the might and dignity of Prince Hector of Troy.

### **The Surviving Achaeans**

Arguably, many of the surviving Achaeans had a more difficult time than Aeneas. Predating the road-trip fiasco movie genre by several millennia, Odysseus had the most famous bad trip of all time. Homer tells of this ill-fated journey in his sequel of sorts to the *Iliad* called the *Odyssey*.

In Homer's *Odyssey*, Odysseus – though still protected by Athena – had angered Poseidon by defeating his favored Trojans. Because the horse ruse was his idea, the god of the sea sent a storm to throw his fleet off course, landing them on the island of the lotus-eaters. Having been fed the magical herb, Odysseus' men forgot where they had come from, what they were doing, and where they were going. Odysseus had to drag them back to their ships, where they were once again sent off course and landed on an island they thought was uninhabited.

There, they found a cave that had stores of meat and cheese, which they ate freely until its inhabitant returned. Polyphemus, a cyclops and a son of Poseidon, discovered the Achaeans eating his food and promptly began eating *them*. He rolled a boulder in front of the mouth of the cave, trapping the Achaeans to their fate. After losing many of his men, Odysseus got the cyclops drunk and blinded him with a wooden stake once he had passed out. Awaking angry and in pain, Polyphemus groped around the cave but could not find the surviving Achaeans, who were sensibly remaining quiet. However, they were still trapped, and Odysseus hatched the plan of attaching themselves to the undersides of the cyclops' sheep he was keeping inside.

Eventually, Polyphemus had to let his sheep out to graze. He inspected each sheep as they passed through to make sure it was, in fact, a sheep, but he failed to thoroughly check their bellies, to which the Achaeans were clinging. In an attempt to hide his deeds from Poseidon, Odysseus halted his escape to call to Polyphemus, telling him that his name was "Nobody" and that all the world would know that *Nobody* had blinded the cyclops.

This is precisely how Polyphemus responded to his father.

"Who blinded you, son?"

"Nobody! Nobody blinded me!"

Odysseus was alternatingly too clever for his good and not nearly as clever as he thought. In this instance, it was a bit of both. Poseidon was a god, after all, and he knew what Odysseus had done to his son. Even more enraged than before, Poseidon agreed to Polyphemus' curse that Odysseus and his crew would wander the seas for ten years before returning to Ithaca. All of Odysseus' fleet but his own ship was soon destroyed, lost, or sunk.

Odysseus and Polyphemus *by Arnold Böcklin. Credit: Wikimedia Commons.*

When they again made landfall, all of Odysseus' men were turned into pigs by Circe when she provided them with drugged cheese and wine. Only Odysseus remained in human form, having been warned by Hermes and given an herb called *moly* that prevented his transformation. Odysseus managed to convince Circe to return his crew to their original forms by agreeing to stay with her as her lover. After a year, with Circe's help, they were able to continue their journey. She told them that if they ate the sacred cattle of Helios on the island of Thrinacia, they would never make it home to Ithaca. She also gave them many warnings of what they were going to encounter. She told them that their journey would take them past the deadly and beautiful sirens of the sea, whose enchanting songs made sailors jump from their ships, seeking the source only to find their own watery graves. Odysseus and his crew prepared for this by jamming beeswax in their ears. That is, all *except for Odysseus*. He ordered his men to tie him to the mast and guard him, but he wanted to hear the song of the sirens for himself. When the time came, Odysseus begged and pleaded to be let down so that he could find the music, but his watchful crew stayed true to their orders and defied him until his wits returned. Afterward, Odysseus boasted that he was the only man ever to hear the sirens and live to tell about it.

Next, their journey took them through narrow straits, where on one side they had to avoid a terrible maelstrom called Charybdis that would suck their ship to the bottom of the sea, and on the other side, they avoided the Scylla, a six-headed monster that fed on passing mariners. Six of the crew were taken, one by each head, before the ship had safely passed. Like many of the obstacles faced in the journey, they probably represented something more realistic but equally deadly.

Shipwrecks were a part of early Mediterranean life. There were many tight squeezes for ships trying to avoid both being pulled into whirlpools or lost in the open sea if they ventured too far from land, risking the unknown shorelines and barely submerged rocks if they got too close.

Regardless, the survivors now sought refuge on the island of Thrinacia. Odysseus advised against this, remembering Circe's warning, but agreed when the rest of his crew urged him to go. Here, Zeus sent a storm that prevented them from leaving for a very long time, and they ate their way through the food that Circe had set them off with. Facing starvation, the crew slaughtered and ate the sacred cattle of Helios while Odysseus was away praying for the storm to end. Helios demanded that they be killed, so Zeus relented the storm for long enough to convince them it was over, only to start it up again while they were at sea. The ship sunk, drowning all the crew except for Odysseus, who washed up on the shore of Ogygia.

Now the lone remainder of his own crew, Odysseus stayed on Ogygia with the nymph Calypso as her lover for seven years. It has been speculated that this was truly all that happened, and the rest was a tale made up by the always (too) clever Odysseus to explain his long absence to his wife, Penelope.

Regardless, by the time he left Ogygia and returned to Ithaca, twenty years had passed since he left and ten since the end of the war. He had been presumed dead, so he showed up to find that many suitors had arrived seeking marriage with his widow. In order to gain information, he disguised himself as an old beggar, a trick that Penelope should have remembered from before the war. He questioned her about the suitors and observed how she responded when he told her that he had met a man named Odysseus on the island of Crete. Once he was convinced that she was still true to him, he revealed himself to his now-grown son, Telemachus. Together, they devised a competition among the suitors that only Odysseus could win, where his bow was strung, and he shot an arrow cleanly through twelve rings. After watching each try and fail, Odysseus, still disguised as a beggar, proves his strength by stringing the bow and sending the arrow flying through the loops.

For the suitors' perceived treachery against Odysseus, he and Telemachus slaughtered them all and even killed many of the palace caretakers who had aided or lain with the would-be grooms.

Odysseus, thanks to his enduring wit, had defied the gods, heard the song of the sirens, bested a cyclops, was the sole survivor of a shipwreck, and was loved by both a sea nymph and a sorceress. Or at least, so he said.

Agamemnon had a less convoluted return to Mycenae than Odysseus had to Ithaca, but it proved more troublesome. He had left his throne as the most powerful of the Achaean kings, but old family troubles had returned in his absence. The feud between his father Atreus and his uncle Thyestes proved to be only temporarily settled as now Aegisthus, the son of Thyestes, had married Agamemnon's wife Clytemnestra and installed himself on the throne. This mirrored Thyestes' affair with Aerope, who was Atreus' wife and Agamemnon's mother.

Clytemnestra had abandoned Agamemnon due to his willingness to sacrifice their daughter, Iphigenia, in the name of his precious war. She took her revenge by conspiring with Aegisthus to murder him, along with Cassandra – who had returned as his concubine. Aegisthus ruled for seven years until the cycle claimed him, too. Agamemnon's son, Orestes, returned from exile and killed both Aegisthus and Clytemnestra (his own mother) for their treachery against his father. In the eyes of justice, Orestes seemed to take one step forward and once step back by avenging his father yet killing his mother. As a result, he was pursued by the Furies, who were goddesses of vengeance and retribution that drove men insane.

Apollo and Athena took his side, though, and Apollo told them that if he went to the barbarous island of Tauris to retrieve a statue of Artemis, he could end the torment of the Furies. He was captured and brought to a priestess, who turned out to be his long-lost sister, Iphigenia, who he had believed to be dead. She told him that Athena had saved her, and then she helped Orestes' escape and found the statue of Artemis. This turn of events broke the cycle of vengeance that had cursed the family, and the Furies stopped their pursuit of Orestes. He returned to Mycenae, took Hermione as his wife (the daughter of Menelaus and Helen), and ruled as king.

This series of unfortunate events that befell Agamemnon and his kin was part of what is called the *Curse of the House of Atreus*. A curse that was "contagious" in ancient Greek mythology was called a *miasma*. It began with Agamemnon's great-grandfather, Tantalus, who tried to trick the gods into eating his son as a test of their omniscience. He was discovered and sent to the underworld where he endured a truly Dante-esque torture for his arrogance. He stood in a pool of water, but every time he bent to take a sip, the water evaporated before he could reach it. Likewise, he was positioned beneath a tree that bore fruit, but if he reached to pick one, a breeze would blow the branch just out of his reach. The miasma spread to his children, where it morphed into fratricide, patricide, incest, and human sacrifice until it was broken by Agamemnon's children, Iphigenia and Orestes.

Other notable Achaeans that survived fared better. Nestor, who did not participate in the looting of Troy, enjoyed a safe and speedy journey home. Eventually, he would leave again to create the colony of Metapontum in southern Italy.

Diomedes made it home to find his wife had moved on without him, so he, too, decided to start a colony in southern Italy.

Philoctetes also joined the Italy club, where he founded a sanctuary for Apollo the Wanderer, dedicating the bow of Herakles that he had carried since his injury and abandonment.

Neoptolemus returned to Phthia with Andromache, where he followed Peleus, his grandfather, as king. The pair had a child named Molossus, and their lineage is said to be traced to Alexander the Great of Macedon. The Macedonian kings also claimed to be descended from Herakles, but it is probably fair to say that what really mattered to them was linking their family to a nearly invincible demi-god, *whichever one that may be.*

However, Ajax the Lesser did not fare well and was almost immediately killed by the gods on his journey home as retribution for his destruction of the Temple of Apollo and the rape of the priestesses. The gods were very inconsistent about when things like arson, rape, slavery, and murder were and were not okay. Mostly, they just did not like Ajax.

# PART THREE: THE IMPACT OF THE TROJAN WAR

# Chapter 10: The Literature: Ancient Greek Writers on the Trojan War

Homer's *Iliad* is the oldest and most complete account of the events surrounding the Trojan War, and his *Odyssey* fleshes out some of the events after the funeral of Hector. In fact, these two books are among the oldest texts in the world that can still be read today. As old as they are, they were still written between four and five hundred years after the events of the Trojan War, a period which not inconsequentially spanned a dark age in Greek history.

What texts or information made it to Homer would have survived through a combination of oral tradition and some scattered records. Homer himself lived in Anatolia, nearer to the site of Ancient Troy than to that of Ancient Mycenae, Athens, or Sparta. This may be both the reason for the seeming sympathies to a Greek enemy in his poems and his access to more information about the events after several hundred years. The *Iliad* and the *Odyssey*, though, were not complete accounts of the conflict.

The *Iliad* is especially paltry, covering less than two months of the ten-year war. At one point in the series of books, the Epic Cycle existed, detailing the whole ordeal from beginning to end in epic dactylic hexameter. In chronological order of the war (though not necessarily in chronological publishing order), these epic poems were *Cypria, Iliad, Aethiopis, Little Iliad, Sack of Troy, Return from Troy, Odyssey,* and *Telegony.* The fragments that have survived from the other books in the Epic Cycle are usually lines that have been found quoted elsewhere, usually by later Greek historians. The original works themselves are lost to history

### Cypria

*Cypria* was written either by Homer, Stasinus of Cyprus, Hegesinus of Salamis, or Cyprias of Halicarnassus. Fifty scattered lines survive, and they tell of the initial events that led to the Trojan War. They describe Zeus' plan to depopulate the world of his demigod children, the judgment of Paris, the gathering of the Achaean forces and the prophecies of Calchas at Aulis, the death of Protesilaus at the hands of Hector, and Greek envoy to negotiate the return of Helen and the treasure stolen by Paris.

### The *Iliad* (see Chapter 6)

### Aethiopis

The third poem in the Epic Cycle was written by Arctinus of Miletus and begins after Achilles' victory over Hector. *Aethiopis* tells the story of the continued challenges faced by the Achaean hero and his insatiable desire to prove that he was the greatest warrior in the world. At least, that is the presumption from its scant five lines that survive about his battles with Penthesilea and Memnon.

### Little Iliad

This epic poem is attributed to either Homer, Lesches of Pyrrha, Cinaethon of Sparta, or Diodorus of Erythrae. Thirty lines of the original text survive, and while not quoted, it is widely referenced by many more texts, making it one of the better-understood works of the Epic Cycle.

It tells the story of the argument between Odysseus and Ajax over Achilles' armor, the prophecies of Helenus after his capture, the infiltration of the Troy by Odysseus and Diomedes to retrieve the Palladium of Troy, the construction of the Trojan horse by Epeius, and the emergence of the Achaean soldiers once inside the walls of Troy. Because this work is often referenced but not always quoted, there are many discrepancies and contradictions, with no single definitive version from its derivative texts. For example, Helenus' prophecy that the Achaeans must retrieve Philoctetes from Lemnos in order to win the war is in some texts given to Calchas. This Philoctetes arrival and the death of Paris earlier in the story and leaves only three prophecies for the Trojan seer to give the Achaeans.

### *Sack of Troy*

The *Sack of Troy* by Arctinus of Miletus backtracks slightly in the narrative to start with the Trojans discovering the Trojan Horse on the beach and debating what to do with it. The death of Laocoon and his sons, the flight of Aeneas and his party, and the fates of the Trojan royal family at the hands of the Achaean conquerors. Only ten lines survive, making this one of the more anemic remnants of the Epic Cycle.

### *Return from Troy*

Written by either Homer, Eumelus of Corinth, or Agias of Troezen, only five and a half lines remain from this contribution to the story. More can be inferred through other texts that do not quote it directly, and its contents told of the stories of most of the Achaeans after the war (save for Odysseus, who gets his own book). The Italian colonies of Nestor, Diomedes, and Philoctetes were covered in this text as well as the murder of Agamemnon and Cassandra at the hands of Aegisthus and Clytemnestra.

*Odyssey* (see chapter 9)

## *Telegony*

The final installment of the Epic Cycle is *Telegony* by Cinaethon of Sparta, and it is a weird finale. It begins with Odysseus and Telemachus burying the bodies of the slain suitors. However, the story shifts to a son that his lover Circe had given birth to after he and his crew left her island. His son, Telegonus, left the island after growing to adulthood, and unwittingly landed in Ithaca when a storm blew his ship off course. Not knowing that he was on his father's land, he began stealing and slaughtering cattle to eat. An aged Odysseus came to defend his property and was abruptly killed by Telegonus in an ensuing fight. Telegonus and Odysseus were able to recognize each other in his final moments, and he lamented what he had done.

Telegonus then found Penelope and his half-brother, Telemachus, and returned to Circe's island. Telegonus married Penelope, Telemachus married Circe, and Circe made all of them immortal. So close to the ultimate conceit of outwitting death, Odysseus died as a mortal while his family lived forever.

During the Classical Age of Athens, Greek dramatists also contributed to the growing cacophony of heroic but often conflicting accounts of the then nearly millennium-old war. For context, a Trojan War play for Classical Athenians was akin to a modern audience watching Robinhood. Still, they were captivated by the characters, who had morphed to become more complex and less brutal over time. The three main dramatists whose works have survived are Aeschylus, Sophocles, and Euripides.

## Aeschylus and the Oresteia Trilogy

Aeschylus is known as the father of Greek tragedy, though only seven of his approximately seventy to ninety plays survived the ravages of time. Despite most of his work being lost to history, three of the seven surviving plays represent a trilogy about the late days of the House of Atreus.

His play *Agamemnon* starts with the titular character's return home from the Trojan War. However, Agamemnon is mostly seen through the eyes of other characters. The townspeople fear the curse on the house and worry about retribution for his sacrifice of Iphigenia. His wife, Clytemnestra, is appalled that he has brought home a Trojan concubine. Cassandra foresees the murder of Agamemnon and herself but walks towards her fate, knowing that no one will believe her, and she will not be able to escape it even if she tries.

In the next book, *The Libation Bearers*, Agamemnon's son, Orestes, meets his sister, Electra, at their father's tomb to plan vengeance against their mother and Aegisthus, whom she has taken as her new husband. They succeed, but the final installment, *The Eumenides,* describes his guilt and the torment inflicted on him by the Furies for his kin slaying. In the end, Orestes is forgiven for his actions against his mother, and the Furies are renamed The Eumenides or *The Kindly Ones*.

## Sophocles: Electra, Ajax, and Philoctetes

While Sophocles is most known for his *Oedipus Rex* and *Antigone* tragedies, he also contributed to the legend of the Trojan War through three of his plays, though these are not a trilogy. His play Ajax attempts to somewhat rescue the reputations of Ajax the Great and Odysseus, who each had some confusing moments in the aftermath of Achilles' death. Electra is another telling of The Libation Bearers where she and Orestes plot the death of their mother and Aegisthus – but with Electra as the protagonist rather than Orestes.

In Sophocles' version, Ajax did not immediately kill himself after Achilles' armor was awarded to Odysseus, but rather swore vengeance upon Agamemnon and Menelaus, who had each voted against him. In a rage, he gathered his weapons and non-Achilles' armor and went in search of the maligned brothers to kill them. However, Athena clouded his vision so that he ended up killing the Greek's cattle and herdsmen instead. When Ajax regained his senses and realized what he had done, the shame drove him to suicide. While this attempts to explain a little bit more about what drove the hero to impale himself, it completely changes the rationale. In the original, he chose death over the dishonor brought on him by the judgment of others. However, in this version, he chose death rather than deal with the disgrace he had brought on himself. Odysseus, for his part, argued to have a proper burial for Ajax despite his recent actions, which Agamemnon and Menelaus reluctantly agreed to. Finally, *Philoctetes* begins with Odysseus and Neoptolemus (instead of Diomedes) going to Lemnos to bring the wounded archer to Troy after languishing for nearly a decade on the island by himself with an oddly festering foot. The morality and motivations behind each of the options play out, as Odysseus and Neoptolemus consider taking the bow and arrows but leaving Philoctetes, and Philoctetes is reluctant to join them ever after learning how the prophecy needs him to return for the Achaeans to win.

## Euripides' Nine Plays

Euripides was the last of the great dramatists of the classical era, and he wrote the most prolifically of the three about the Trojan War. His nine surviving plays about the war are Andromache (wife of Hector), Hecuba (wife of King Priam during the Trojan War), Cyclops, Electra (daughter of King Agamemnon and Queen Clytemnestra of Mycenae), The Trojan Women, Iphigenia in Tauris, Helen, Orestes, and Iphigenia in Aulis.

### Andromache

At the palace of Neoptolemus, Orestes sees his friend Pylades. Neoptolemus is shielding Astyanax in order to earn favor with Andromache, so the Greeks have dispatched him to fetch him. Orestes, who is madly in love with Hermione, makes his requests to Neoptolemus, who snubs them. But his refusal is conditioned on Andromache's love. Hermione intends to return to King Menelaus, her father.

Okay, stay with me here...

Neoptolemus, irritated by Andromache's coldness, concedes to Orestes. Enraged at the course of events, Orestes organizes the kidnapping of Hermione. After failing to persuade Hermione to preserve her son, Andromache turns to Neoptolemus, who wants her hand in marriage in exchange for his protection.

Andromache resolves to succumb to Neoptolemus after consulting Hector's spirit at his tomb but prepares to murder herself immediately after the wedding ceremony. Hermione demands that Orestes kill Neoptolemus at the altar in retaliation for Neoptolemus' rejection. Hermione is torn furiously between love and hate after Neoptolemus' departure. When Cleone, her confidante, informs her of Neoptolemus' insulting happiness at the wedding ceremony, resentment wins over. When she hears Orestes' narrative of how the Greeks avenged her by killing Neoptolemus at the altar, she curses him and stabs herself in the body of Neoptolemus. Orestes is overcome by despair, followed by lunacy.

(True to their reputation, Greek and Roman mythology reads like episodes of the late 70s television show, SOAP.)

### *Hecuba*

The Greeks have conquered Troy. The women of Troy have been divided among the Achaean victors, but they have returned home. Strong winds are holding up the Greek fleet. The ghost of Achilles has requested the sacrifice of Polyxena was the daughter of Hecuba and Priam, Troy's ruler. Odysseus, the Greek hero, arrives to take her away. He was unmoved by Hecuba's anguish or her reminder that he once owed her his life. On the other hand, Polyxena would rather die than be enslaved, and she accepts her fate. Hecuba is bereaved yet again as she prepares for the burial. Polydorus, her youngest son, had been sent with a portion of Priam's fortune to Polymestor, ruler of the Thracian Chersonese (where the Greek fleet is now held).

When Troy fell, Polymestor murdered the youngster, Polydorus, and threw his body into the sea to capture the treasure for himself. It has been washed and transported to Hecuba. She seeks retribution from Agamemnon, the Greek king, but he is cautious, despite his sympathies. Hecuba then takes matters into her own hands and seeks vengeance. Polymestor and his boys are lured to her tent, where her servants slit his eyes and murder his sons. Agamemnon sends the blinded king to a secluded island and prophesies that Hecuba would change into a dog for what she has done.

## *Cyclops*

This is an oddly familiar take on the more common version of Odysseus' encounter with the cyclops in the *Odyssey*. Here, Odysseus visits his friend, Silenus, on Mount Etna in Sicily and offers him food in exchange for his wine. As a Dionysiac servant, Silenus cannot help himself from obtaining the wine, despite the fact that the food is not his to liking. Cyclops arrives shortly after, and Silenus accuses Odysseus of taking the food, vowing to the gods and the nearby Satyrs that he is telling the truth.

Cyclops takes Odysseus and his crew inside his cave after a dispute and consumes some of them. Odysseus manages to escape and is taken aback by what he sees. He devises a plan to get the cyclops drunk and then burn off his eye with a big poker while he is unconscious.

When Cyclops gets inebriated, he claims to be seeing gods and begins referring to Silenus as Ganymede. The Cyclops then kidnaps Silenus and takes him to his cave, and Odysseus begins the next stage of his plan. When the time comes, Odysseus enlists the help of the Satyrs, who burn out the cyclops' eye. His name was "Noman," as he had informed the Cyclops before. As a result, when the Cyclops cries out who blinded him, it sounds like he is saying, *"No Man blinded me."*

## *Trojan Women*

One of Euripides' most moving tragedies, this play depicts the predicament of the Trojan women after their men have been slaughtered and they are at the mercy of their Achaean captives. They wait for their fate, sad and worried. The herald, Talthybius, says that they will be divided among the victorious. The Trojan queen Hecuba will fall into the hands of the despised Odysseus; her daughter Cassandra will be given to Agamemnon, and her other daughter Polyxena will be slain on Achilles' grave.

Cassandra, the tragic figure, appears. As a prophetess, she foretells the conqueror's doom, but, as usual, no one listens or believes her. Andromache arrives with her son, Astyanax, to be the prize of Achilles' son, Neoptolemus. Talthybius reappears to abduct Astyanax, who has been sentenced to death by the Greeks.

Menelaus and Helen meet next; Menelaus is hell-bent on destroying her, and Hecuba fuels his hatred. On the other hand, Helen pleads her case, and their reconciliation is hinted at when Helen and Menelaus depart. Talthybius reappears with Astyanax's broken body, and Hecuba prepares the funeral. Troy is set on fire, and the city's towers crumble as the women flee into slavery.

## *Iphigenia in Aulis*

When Iphigenia was going to be sacrificed at Aulis, Artemis interfered and substituted her with a deer on the altar, sparing the girl and whisking her away to Tauris. There, she became a priestess in the temple of Artemis, where she must ritually sacrifice foreigners who land on King Thoas' coasts.

Iphigenia despises her forced religious slavery in Tauris and is desperate to let her family know she is still alive. In addition, she had a premonition about her brother, Orestes, which leaves her feeling that he had died. Meanwhile, Orestes has murdered his mother, Clytemnestra, and is enraged by the Furies. Despite the fact that he was judged not guilty in Athens, some Furies continue to hunt him. As a result, Apollo orders him to take a sacred statue of Artemis and return it to Athens, where he will be set free. As per local custom, he is arrested by Taurian guards and taken to the temple, where they will be executed.

Orestes and Iphigenia recognize each other and rejoice, and Iphigenia tricks King Thoas into letting Orestes live by telling him that her brother's matricide has contaminated the Artemis statue. She recommends letting them both go, as she has disgraced herself and is also disgraced through her family. They flee while King Thoas is still deciding, bringing the statue with them. Thoas pledges to track down and slay the fugitives, but Athena intervenes and allows them to escape.

## *Helen*

Helen never ran away to Troy with Paris in this alternate history but rather was carried away to Egypt, where King Proteus safeguarded her. After Proeteus' death, his son Theoclymenos planned to marry Helen, who remained faithful to her husband, Menelaus. When news reached Egypt that Menelaus had drowned, Helen became eligible for marriage. To be certain, she visited the king's sister, Theonoe, who was a seer. She learns that Menelaus survived and that a stranger would soon arrive in Egypt. This stranger turned out to be none other than Menelaus himself! Needing to find a way out of Egypt, she told King Theoclymenos that Menelaus was, in fact, dead and that she needed to perform a burial at sea in order to be free to marry him. Menelaus, still in disguise, snuck onto the boat with her, and they fled back to Greece.

## *Electra*

In Euripides' telling of *Electra*, she was married off to a farmer because she was afraid that if she stayed in the royal household and married a noble, their children would try to avenge Agamemnon's death one day. Electra resented her exile and her mother's dedication to Aegisthus, despite his kindness towards her. Orestes, the son of Agamemnon and Clytemnestra, was fully exiled and sent to the king of Phocis, where he became friends with the king's son Pylades.

Once grown, Orestes and Pylades returned to Mycenae in search of vengeance and found Electra and her husband. Despite trying to conceal their identities in order to gain information, a servant recognized Orestes by a scar. Electra agreed to help her brother on his mission of revenge. They decide to lure Clytemnestra away from the house so that Orestes could kill Aegisthus. Having done so, they struggled over the decision of killing their mother. In this version, both Orestes and Electra kill their mother together and are both immediately torn by guilt. Shades appear to tell them that although their mother deserved her death, they had still committed a shameful act for which they must atone.

## *Orestes*

Orestes and Electra had fled to Sparta in search of Menelaus' protection after Clytemnestra's murder. Helen emerged from the palace under the guise of making an offering at her sister Clytemnestra's grave, blaming Apollo for the House of Atreus' misfortunes. Orestes awakened after Helen had left, still enraged by the Furies. When Menelaus arrived at the palace, he and Orestes talked about the murder and the torment that followed them ever since. Tyndareus, Orestes' grandfather, and Menelaus' father-in-law entered and discussed humanity's interference in divine justice.

Later, Orestes and Pylades argued their case in front of the town assembly, but Orestes and Electra were sentenced to death. In an interesting turn, they decide to plot against Menelaus, Helen, and Hermione, who they feel have now wronged them. Helen vanished into thin air when the siblings went to kill her, so they moved next to Hermione. Menelaus entered just in time, and before more bloodshed could occur, Apollo appeared to inform Menelaus that Helen had been set among the stars and that Orestes must stand trial in Athens. He assured Orestes that he would be acquitted and that he was to marry Hermione.

## *Iphigenia and Aulis*

The play opens with Agamemnon already having agreed to sacrifice his daughter, Iphigenia, in order to appease Artemis, but he is beginning to have second thoughts. He attempts to send a letter to her to turn around and return to Mycenae, but Menelaus intercepted it before it could reach her and leans into a fierce argument with his brother for changing his mind.

Strangely, as a result of the debate, each brother wins by changing the other's mind, and they switch sides! Menelaus would now prefer to disband the Achaean force and give up on retrieving his wife rather than see his innocent niece die, and Agamemnon strengthened his resolve that the sacrifice was painful but necessary to their cause. Still in disagreement, neither brother manages to warn Clytemnestra to turn back, so they arrive in the camp believing that Iphigenia was coming there to marry Achilles. This ruse was short-lived and served primarily to infuriate Achilles. As Agamemnon's wife and daughter learn the truth, they are terrified and argue with Agamemnon, who is by now completely convinced that it is the right thing to do. Achilles was ready to defend Iphigenia, but the girl agreed to be sacrificed when she saw how it was tearing apart the Achaean army to stay there with no wind to carry them to Troy. At the very last moment, Artemis had mercy and switched the girl for a deer.

Yes, these versions are very different – but such is mythology. Through generations of telling and re-telling – combined with cultural changes requiring a change in the narrative – these stories become somewhat of a Frankenstein; bits and pieces substituted here and there, and occasionally, an entirely foreign element is added. And while many are difficult to follow, the resounding themes are ones of plotting, revenge, escape, and forgiveness.

# Chapter 11: The Legend: How Ancient Greeks Viewed the Trojan War

This chapter will cover the period when the *Iliad* and the *Odyssey* were written, how they were passed from generation to generation, what the Ancient Greeks believed about the war (whether it was a myth or not), and *when it took place* according to the ancient scholars.

Much debate still rages about the lines that historians and scholars should draw between the history, religion, and outright entertainment present in these stories. But what about the Greeks themselves? How much stock did they put into their own stories, and how much – if any – did they greet with an eye roll and/or dismiss as embellishment?

There is obviously no single correct answer to this question.

Like people today, the Ancient Greeks were not a monolith. The myths of the Ancient Greeks were firmly embedded within their culture. While many may have taken their stories quite literally, others sought them out for their metaphors, poetry, and punchlines. For the Greeks who lived during Homer's time, Classical Athens, or the empire of Alexander the Great, the Trojan War was ancient. The city of Troy had gone, and the Achaean Greeks bore little resemblance to their modern Greek culture. As seen through the dramas of Aeschylus, Sophocles, and Euripides, much of the tweaking of the stories was to humanize the characters and align them more with their fifth-century BCE values.

So, the question becomes more complicated: not only, "Did the Greeks believe their stories *literally*?" but also, "Which versions of their myths were most believed and disbelieved, and how did that change over time?" There is perhaps a better way to approach this question obliquely, and that is to ask, "What did the Greeks think about their heroes?" This is a far more relatable and far more answerable question.

After all, it is not silly to ask people what they think about Luke's journey in Star Wars or debate what makes Thor and Steve Rogers "worthy" in the Avengers franchise. They reflect values, and these values can really get historians into the heads of the Ancient Greeks. The Greek myths about the Trojan War were a conversation that everyone could have with one another; not like a language, but like a consciousness.

So, let us dig deep into a few of the characters (or *historical figures* – if that is your belief).

Regardless of which one is used, what is important is that to Ancient Greeks, they represented *archetypes*. Achilles, Odysseus, Hector, Agamemnon, and Helen all stood for something that they more or less agreed on, even if that "something" was subject to some evolution over time. Their stories are about many things, but they revolve around the character's representation of an ideal, and how their nature is both often excused and ultimately leads to their downfall.

*Achilles*

Achilles was clearly everything that a Bronze Age Greek man was supposed to be and is, therefore, the archetypal hero of the war. He is strong, fast, and skilled in battle. Though not overly bright, he was no brute and remained his own man during the Trojan War, commanding his own Myrmidons and frequently asserting his independence, causing Agamemnon and other Greek leaders to continuously court him to the battlefield.

He was also handsome, and he had a strong sense of justice. Sometimes that sense of justice came in the form of traditional fairness, like when he was prepared to defend Iphigenia from her forced sacrifice. Sometimes, however, that came in the form of absolute rage and the irrational justice that was exhibited when he required not only the death of Hector by his own hand but also his eternal humiliation for killing his lifelong companion, Patroclus. The reader is aware that Hector did little wrong in his slaying of Patroclus in battle, but still, the vengeance of Achilles is terrible. This marks one of the lesser discussed aspects of the archetypal hero; *they get people to make exceptions for them.*

The actions of Achilles did not diminish his standing in either Greek or modern minds. Greeks especially knew the end of the story and did not abandon their idyllic warrior when he dragged Hector behind his chariot and left his body for the dogs. For that matter, his status does not drop when he casually sacrifices people to the gods, as he did after the death of Patroclus, or kidnaps and rapes local women, as he did at the beginning of the *Iliad*.

Agamemnon is held accountable for these things, though. In fact, his sacrifice of Iphigenia and his abduction of Cassandra as his concubine are the two main reasons Clytemnestra turned against him in Aeschylus' Oresteia trilogy. Repeatedly throughout the tales of Achilles, his arrogance is explained away by Homer as him just being "great in his greatness." This is both a fancy way of saying he is an archetype for greatness and hinting at the final aspect that makes his archetype complete: his downfall.

While he is the one person in history who literally had an Achilles heel (a phrase now used synonymously with someone's weakness or downfall), this small, unknown vulnerability was not what truly killed him. For characters like Achilles to remain in the collective consciousness, there must be a complete circle. In other words, if he is great because of his greatness, his greatness must also undo him. This aspect of the story is what makes Achilles' story memorable.

He was presented with the choice of being the greatest warrior in the world but dying young or living a long, happy life but being forgotten. He was also given repeated opportunities to turn around – even after making his initial choice to face greatness and death in the Trojan War.

In Greek myths, prophecies are typically law, but Achilles' situation is somewhat unique in the sense that he is essentially given two prophecies that he must choose between. The debate may still go on about whether he really had a choice (given his nature), but it remains a narrative choice not typical for the genre. His duels with Penthesilea and Memnon – after he slew Hector – further illustrate that near the end of his life, proving his greatness has become more of an obsession or a compulsion than a virtue to him.

Having made his choice to be a warrior, he becomes a slave to that choice, even when warned yet again of his impending death if he were to make a certain choice, this time choosing to fight and kill Memnon. Of course, the great warrior hero cannot die by being bested in battle, so his long-foreseen death comes at the hands of what is essentially an assassin in the form of Paris. Further, Paris needs poison on his arrow and the guidance of Apollo to kill Achilles in a way that he did not know he was vulnerable and therefore had not prepared for. In dying this way, all that he was is preserved.

### Odysseus

That hero at the end of the war is undoubtedly Odysseus. Though he possessed many qualities of other Greek heroes, such as skill in battle, he represents a different archetype: the *maverick*. By making his cleverness and quick thinking his greatest attribute, he becomes an important representation of the strategy (and often ruthlessness) needed to be victorious through the theft of the Palladium of Troy and the ruse of the Trojan horse.

Through Odysseus, Greeks saw the flaws of brute strength and conventional mores. While duty binds Hector to meet his almost assured death by single combat, Odysseus has no qualms about stealth, backstabbing, and the brutal murder of Hector's child. As Ajax chooses death over dishonor when he is passed over for Achilles' armor, Odysseus is very comfortable with dishonorable actions such as lying and cheating so long as it means he wins.

Lastly, the shift to Odysseus contrasts Achilles by choosing a different representation of his glory: his survival. Where Achilles needed to die in order to be great, Odysseus needed to live. His *Odyssey* ends with him as the sole survivor of the voyage home to Ithaca, and the lone suitor of Penelope left standing.

As already detailed, the cleverness of Odysseus and his need to survive are in his nature, and much of his unsavory behavior is forgiven in that context. His murder of Astyanax, the child son of Hector and Andromache, is explained away because it would prevent future vengeance and further war against the Greeks. His complete abandonment of Philoctetes (almost twice) on Lemnos was also forgiven, as he did it in the name of Greek victory and prevention of plague, perhaps even leprosy, among the Achaean armies. Even the deaths of his entire crew are justified to show both their lack of caution and Odysseus' talent for survival.

Like Achilles, Odysseus was not killed by having been bested in his own strengths but through an *unknown weakness*. His lack of knowledge about his son through Circe led to a miscalculation of who

– and how dangerous – the cattle-stealing stranger he met in Ithaca truly was. Left to an unplanned conventional fight many years past his physical prime, Odysseus was killed.

It is also notable that Odysseus was only able to be killed once he stopped adventuring and settled down. In other words, he died when he *stopped* being who he was. Where Achilles would have faced a symbolic death by being forgotten had he decided to settle down, Odysseus met his literal death by doing so, further contrasting the two Homeric heroes of the *Iliad* and *Odyssey*, respectively.

## Hector

Hector is the honorable protector of the Trojan War epic. While he possesses mostly the same physical traits and skills as Achilles, he uses them to defend his family and his people rather than to seek glory or remembrance. This honorable trait was first seen in his decision to back his brother, Paris, despite thinking of him as a fool and disagreeing with what he had done. His strength as a warrior is honed and focused by this loyalty, which gives him the power to fight the Achaeans for a decade over something that he agreed with them about. This is how Homer (and the Greeks who read his work) were able to relate to the enemy side of the battle; he did not make them antagonists; he made them contrasting archetypes.

The *Iliad* and the *Odyssey* are stories that have no true antagonists, except for prophecies and perhaps the gods and goddesses. Therefore, the Greeks could get behind Hector and feel conflicted over the principles and outcome of the war in favor of the Achaeans, their own ancestors. It allowed Hector to become a *rival*, or honorable foe, to the Greek cause. He represented many of their own values, simply on the other side of the wall, rather than being a *nemesis* that was seen as their opposite.

And much like his Greek counterparts, much violence was done in the name of his loyalty and honor that the audience is encouraged to overlook. Defending his brother's actions that he knows to be wrong is perhaps his cruelest act towards the city of Troy. In essence, he is more willing to be honorable than to be right, and the nature of Hector is perhaps the most tragic because it leads not only to his own downfall but to the senseless deaths of thousands. He fights the Achaeans on principle, which is something that the two other heroes would have never done.

Thus, this trio competes for the crown of who the "true" hero of the Trojan War was, which is the most important part of the stories for the Greeks. Whether they believed that Achilles was a demi-god or simply an incredibly fast and skilled warrior is far less important than whether they believed that made him superior to Odysseus and Hector.

Similarly, who they were more likely to excuse for their faults and bad behavior demonstrates the archetype they associate with more strongly. If impetuousness and vanity can be overlooked by someone being the absolute best at what they do, then that is a vote for Achilles. If ruthlessness and deceit are forgivable when they are accompanied by cunning and big-picture planning, then Odysseus is the protagonist of choice. And if the sacrifice and death of the masses can be justified by the principle for which one fights, then Hector is the central figure of the saga. There are also other important characters who, while not seen as the saga's ultimate heroes, are important for understanding Ancient Greek thinking about the Trojan War.

*Agamemnon*

The most powerful Achaean king and the leader of the Greek armies for the duration of the Trojan War is not among the central heroes but is still prominent in Greek thinking as the archetype for a ruler and (absent) father. Even the House of Atreus; curse, while named after his father and begun by his great-grandfather, runs through Agamemnon. Tantalus, Pelops, and Atreus are described as his ancestors, and Orestes, Electra, and Iphigenia are his children, making him the focal point of his own family's saga within the events of the Trojan War.

As the ruler archetype, he puts his own power ahead of his family, which was most exemplified by his willingness to sacrifice Iphigenia, even if he waffled for a while. The action was needed in order for the Achaeans to set sail for Troy, and the defeat of Troy was needed to make Agamemnon and Mycenae the main seat of power in the Aegean regions. All of this was done at the expense of his family, which makes it significant that his house's curse is related to a lack of loyalty to one's own family. The cycle of vengeance and murder among their own kin is what consistently brings about their suffering, and it only ends when his son Orestes is mournful and seeks forgiveness for killing his mother.

Agamemnon's nature was to seek power, and while he is the only one of his kin that does not literally kill a member of his own family (on a technicality), he was certainly willing to do so and did so symbolically through his neglect and absence. There was no sense of family in his actions, which is a direct contrast to Hector, who would have inherited the Trojan throne and been considered the most powerful leader of the Aegean's had his defense of his family and people been successful.

Agamemnon, victorious, returns home only to be killed just as he achieves the height of his power. While containing the same sort of tragic flaw as the other heroes, Agamemnon is not granted the same forgiveness by the audience. He is widely seen as going too far and letting his ambition get the better of him and is a cautionary tale rather than one to emulate or admire. This downfall sets him apart from the heroic trio of Achilles, Odysseus, and Hector.

### Helen

Another cautionary tale is that of Helen, though it is a far different kind than that of Agamemnon. Her story begins in Sparta with Menelaus winning a competition for her betrothal, which was granted by her father, King Tyndareus. At no point did she choose Menelaus, though many revisions of her story, such as those of Euripides, try to make her more loyal to her first husband. Nor did she really choose

Paris, either, as she was promised to him not by her father but by the goddess Aphrodite for naming her the victor in a contest of beauty. In order to enforce the "prize," Helen was shot by a magical arrow of Eros (later Cupid, to the Romans) so that she would run off with Paris to Troy. When it comes to Helen, interpretation is very important and divergent, which is what makes her one of the most controversial and enigmatic figures in the epic. Like the three heroes, the way that the Greeks chose to see Helen betrayed their own values, just as it is in today's society.

For those that believe Helen was a dutiful wife who was manipulated and enchanted by the gods to make her run off and act against her nature, she represents the Jungian archetype of the "Everyman." *(Or, in this case, the "Everywoman.")* It is not so much that she has a character of her own making, as it is that she provides an entry point into the story for the audience and a justification for the war that follows. This interpretation is supported by the continued treatment of Helen as a bargaining chip, starting with her betrothal to Menelaus and following her to Troy, where a group of men discuss her as property of her husband (whichever one they side with) and then make decisions on her behalf. It was not her choice to marry Menelaus, it was not her choice to fall in love with Paris, and it was not her choice to stay in Troy or return to Sparta.

*A depiction of Helen. Credit: Wikimedia Commons.*

The second interpretation is the Helen married Menelaus because it was expected of her as a princess of Sparta, but that she truly fell in love with Paris and decided to leave with him of her own accord. This reading turns Helen into the archetype of the lover, who seeks happiness, intimacy, and experience above all else. Supporting this is the description of Helen as the most beautiful woman in the world, rather than the most dutiful. While she could certainly be both, the emphasis on the former holds it as the most important and implies that she would seek the beauty and intimacy in others rather than simply doing what was expected of her. The fact that she and Paris are at odds with one another further supports this view since a dutiful wife would have supported him no matter what went on in the Ancient Aegean world. She falls out of love with Paris over their dispute, which would be more consistent with a passionate personality and more likely than the magic of the gods suddenly wearing off. This would also make her downfall in keeping with that of the other characters. If her passionate nature led her to run off, it was also likely to lead to death and destruction, and her eventual return to a loveless and imprisoning marriage to Menelaus in Sparta would be a suitably tragic fate.

A final interpretation of her character is that she was a true actor in the events of the war and played both sides for an outcome that was for her own betterment. In this narrative, she would have taken the archetype of the magician, the type of person that catalyzes change and seeks the improvement of their station through their own initiative. Her betrothal was not necessarily a bad thing, especially since her betrothed was something of a dimwit – and the union would allow her to remain in Sparta.

However, through Paris' diplomatic visits to Sparta, Helen at some point came to believe that Troy held better promise for her. Perhaps it could have been because she believed them more powerful, or because she saw an opportunity to compound her wealth by running off to Troy with Sparta's fortune stowed in the ships, or because there was more equity for women in politics and society – or *all of the above*.

This version does not exclude love, power, wealth, or equity as motivations but requires some leaps about Trojan culture. The latter option is especially interesting, as Andromache is seen as a valuable advisor to Hector, and the Amazons of central Asia figure prominently as fierce warriors on the level of their male counterparts. Still, they are not very large leaps. Homer and the Greek dramatists wrote their stories after hundreds of years of dark ages, and even Classical Greece in its golden age was not so golden for women. It is not difficult to imagine that Helen would have been more of her own agent than the later Greeks were able to grasp properly.

Helen would have needed to change sides back to the Achaeans as her better bet at a certain point in the war. The deaths of Hector, Penthesilea, and Memnon could likely have been the impetus for the change, which is confirmed by her assistance to Odysseus when he and Diomedes entered the city to steal the Palladium. If the symbolic rather than the literal translation of the theft of the Palladium is used, then that means that the ally who showed the Achaeans how to breach the walls could have been Helen rather than Antenor. If she's given even the slightest bit of agency, she is the more obvious choice since she had recently been widowed by the death of Paris and is mentioned explicitly in the tale for helping with the theft of Troy's protective charm. Her final manipulation of Menelaus, who she convinces to take her back rather than kill her, is her final victory, though a tainted one as she would have been a visionary deprived of her dreams of autonomy and forced to rule by stroking the ego of a powerful dope for the rest of her life.

Carl Jung wrote about many of these archetypes in the twentieth century, but it is not revisionism to apply his thinking to people who lived thousands of years before him. He was, after all, trying to get at something that was universal. This was the same thing that the Greeks were doing with their myths and histories, regardless of the overlap between the two genres. So, did the Greeks believe that the Trojan War was real? Yes, obviously. And no, of course not.

# Chapter 12: The Legacy: Modern-Day Findings and Interpretations

In the absence of much convincing archaeological evidence, the city of Troy was believed to have existed in the area referred to as the "Troad," found in northwest Turkey on contemporary maps. Enthusiasts, fascinated by the Homeric legends or the later works of the Greek dramatists, would frequently embark on pilgrimages so they could stand on the same shore that Achilles spilled so much blood on and that Hector gave his life to defend. It was not until the late nineteenth century, though, that there was much to support this until an unlikely duo took their copies of Homer and their spades to Asia Minor.

Frank Calvert lived in the Troad near Hissarlik Hill. He was not a professional archaeologist but had enough knowledge to be effective in his archaeological work. His research led him to believe that this was a good place to begin his dig, and in 1868 recruited another enthusiast-turned archaeologist named Heinrich Schliemann to dig alongside him. Their findings were staggering and took the world by storm. Despite being amateurs, they unearthed ancient heroes along with ancient walls and shards of pottery and brought legitimacy to the nascent discipline of archaeology. Upon finding jewelry, Schliemann famously speculated that he had found the accouterments of the fabled Helen. A new generation inspired by the legends of Homer was soon to take up their torch and carry it into modern times to answer one of history's most nagging questions: Was the Trojan War real?

The excavations began to show that Troy had been occupied, in one form or another, since around 3,000 BCE. They lived in a difficult area that often would have made life challenging for its inhabitants. Archaeological evidence supports that both war and natural disasters such as earthquakes were responsible for the ebbs and flows of Trojan power. In times of affluence and power, such conditions led the Trojans to build fortresses to protect themselves and to store food against the threat of famine or siege. In fact, northwestern Turkey would have been one of the most heavily trafficked bottlenecks in antiquity, and its strategic position at the entrance to the Dardanelles would likely have been utilized to grow their wealth through trade and tariffs. They would, of course, need military strength to make payment a more sensible option than war for the traders and fleets passing through. Setting up a marketplace at this crossroads would have also been of great interest to them, as such win-win profitability would have further discouraged war and violence as a viable strategy, much like modern economic arrangements among EU member states have disincentivized a third world war.

*What is left of Troy's temple to Athena. This temple would have been constructed after the Trojan War. Credit: Carole Raddato, Wikimedia Commons.*

The archaeological record, though, is not one of constant growth. It shows periods of expansions and contractions as their population swelled in times of prosperity and hunkered down through more destructive or deprived cycles. The arrow of time, though, moves just one way. In archaeological terms, this means "up." The deeper the artifacts, walls, or evidence, the longer ago it happened. Troy was rebuilt not in the same place, but each on top of the last one. This stratification, along with tools such as carbon dating, has given archaeologists a pretty good idea of when Troy was strong, weak, or in between. The naming convention has been to use Roman numerals to label from the bottom up, so the oldest settlement of Troy is Troy I, the second oldest Troy II, and so on.

Troy I was small but prosperous, and by the time it had grown into Troy II from 2550 through 2300 BCE, it had become very wealthy for its size, as evidenced by the quality of materials and living conditions compared to their contemporaries. The construction of the city's first walls marks the transition from Troy I to Troy II, with a citadel built on Troy's famous strategic hill, one hundred feet above the surrounding plain.

Still, even with this feature as a constant, much of the rest of the topography would have looked different. The biggest difference from today is that the city would have been much closer to the sea than it is today due to the accumulation of silt in river deltas that have pushed the shoreline further and further away. Its position directly on the shore was significant, as it allowed the city to be by the sea while maintaining a strategic location along land routes. In a lot of ways, Troy was an early version of what the city, now called Istanbul, would be (the city was first called Byzantium, then Constantinople, and finally, Istanbul.) A further advantage for the Trojans came from the nature of sea travel in their day, which saw ships often need to port for days or weeks while they waited for favorable winds. Providing safe harbor and lodging for them would have created a captive market and contributed to their reputation as a trading hub.

By the late Bronze Age – when the Achaeans showed up – Troy had grown grander and wealthier than the inhabitants of Troy II would have believed. In fact, evidence suggests three things. First, that Troy was larger than historians expected. Second, that the descriptions of Troy by Homer were likely highly accurate. And third, *it was likely the largest city Bronze Age city in the Mediterranean.* Troy VII was the final iteration of the city that would be burned and leveled by the Greek forces, but the evidence increasingly shows that the Achaeans came at a bad time. Troy was at its absolute peak, undimmed by any kind of dark age, drought, recent war, or recession. In fact, as time goes on and the slow unearthing of the city continues and even accelerates with modern technology, there is an increasingly strong argument that the Achaeans were scrappy underdogs who had no business taking on such an important center of commerce. Sparta, by comparison, looks more and more like a backwater that Helen may have been fleeing in order to live her life in a more cosmopolitan and fulfilling civilization. Troy was not just a citadel but a city-scale complex with outer and inner walls protecting not just the royalty and nobility – but the entire population. This growth and the movement of the walls further out to encompass the lower town marks the city's final transition, from Troy VII to Troy VIII.

The larger agricultural area had been carefully cultivated under the protection of Troy's military might and the leadership of Hector, who was nicknamed the "Tamer of Horses." This also implies that much of the Trojans' wealth came from horse husbandry. Domesticated horses bred for war were much less common in the late Bronze Age than they would be even by the time of Classical Greece and were therefore that much more valuable. Sheep farming was the foundation for a burgeoning textile industry centered in Troy, which they exported all around the Mediterranean and Asia Minor through their dual access and control of water and land routes. All these details have been recent revelations, as modern equipment has allowed for an analysis of the artifacts not available to the archaeologists even of the twentieth century.

These revelations paint a slightly different picture against the backdrop of the main Aegean powers of the Bronze Age: the Achaeans, the Trojans, and the Hittites. While the assessment of the Hittites as the mightiest of the three has remained unchanged, the leveling of the Achaeans and Trojans might be in the process of revision. Troy's actual territory was small, yes, but the increasing evidence of their prosperity, power, and influence has raised many an eyebrow. It may be that the Achaeans saw this and realized two things.

First, if left unchecked, their "friendly rival" could soon outpace them. Troy's neutrality between the Greeks and Hittites had allowed them to grow to a problematic point. If they did not do something soon, the Achaeans could quickly have two powerful enemies on their hands. By this interpretation, the Trojan War occurred at the height of Trojan power for that exact reason: they were a dangerous ascending power that needed to be kept in check. History has taught nothing if not that leaders prefer the status quo, and Troy was about to disrupt that for the Achaean kingdoms.

In addition, or perhaps extending this line of thinking, the Achaeans may have been driven by greed. Seeing the wealth and power that Troy had accumulated through their strategic position, they coveted the land that they sat on and saw the growth of their own power if they were able to control it. This line of thought provides a much sounder geopolitical explanation for why Achaean leaders other than Menelaus would have gone to war. Agamemnon, perhaps, could have been bound by loyalty to his brother, but loyalty was also not a trait commonly held by the cutthroat members of the House of Atreus. All of this is supported by Hittite tablets that refer to a war around 1180 BCE between the Wilusa, their name for the Trojans, and the Ahhiyawa, their name for the Achaeans.

For some counterevidence as an antidote for getting carried away and claiming proof, Troy was not alone in the Aegean world for its fall around 1180 BCE. For reasons that remain unclear, most of the Mediterranean powers descended into dark ages and ruin around this time, including the Achaeans and Hittites. It was a large reset button, and the "Greeks" who emerged from the dark age around Homer's time were ethnically and culturally different from the Achaeans, even if they still shared a common or related language.

Similarly, the "Hittites" of Asia Minor in the Bronze Age are not the same Hittites that are likely the ancestors of the biblical Hebrews. Troy, as has been documented thoroughly, was hit the hardest. The title of "most strategically located city" passed to Byzantium, and the only way to see a rebuilding of Troy is to place it in Lavinium with the resettlement of Aeneas in Italy, though the historicity of that legend is suspect at best.

Had the Achaeans been more able to capitalize on their victory, historians would likely know more. But after being sacked by the Achaeans, Troy was not rebuilt as a *Greek city*.

Archaeology indicates plenty of trade with the Greek kingdoms but does not place it as Greek itself in any of its iterations. Had there been a Trojan War and had a city as powerful as the one described by Homer been sacked by the Achaeans, there should be some evidence that they attempted to control and resettle the city and its surrounding lands. Perhaps the strangest and least believable part of the Epic Cycle is that everyone just went home after the war or resettled in Italy.

Why Italy? If Nestor, Diomedes, or Philoctetes were looking to start new colonies, why abandon the incredibly lucrative one they had just conquered. In the end, something just does not smell right. What seems most likely is that Homer and the epic poets were left with the same question. What happened in the Mediterranean world after the Trojan War? Some cataclysmic event would have explained the synchronized drop-off, but evidence for such a thing is still wanting. Still, if the authors of the Epic Cycle were indeed left without source material or a clear idea of what happened, then it makes sense that they would try to look forward rather than backward. Expansion into the western Mediterranean was the new frontier of Archaic and Classical Greece, so sending their heroes into the "new world" made more sense than having them vanish with the rest of the old.

These questions – and others – leave historians in an odd place regarding the Trojan War. There is overwhelming archaeological evidence that the city itself not only existed but existed to the standard described by Homeric legend. Yes, the ensuing dark age wiped out any evidence that could have existed about whether such a war between the Achaeans and that civilization was real or invented. That said, Greek historians, poets, and dramatists have proven themselves to be oddly dependable over time, despite their frequent inclusion of the supernatural.

As a result, most historians do believe that war occurred between the Achaeans and the Trojans, a war that is supported by contemporary Hittite texts and the stories of later Greeks. Still, the scale of the war, its participants, and its outcome remains in question by many skeptics. It seems to them too unlikely that such a massive war occurred without leaving a trace of direct evidence beyond a few scant lines of Aramaic and a city that fell into ruin at the same time that many other cities also fell into ruin. These more conservative historians will allow for a short war of an unknown outcome and significance to take place, and that both civilizations fell into ruin shortly afterward.

Still, it is important to gather all that we can out of the emerging archaeological evidence. The ruins that are being exposed and studied through modern excavations could indeed have withstood a ten-year siege, especially if the invading army were not large enough to completely surround the city, a detail corroborated by Epic Cycle texts. Additionally, the battles and technology described are consistent with Homer's tales, though this could always be ascribed to the poet's own understanding of history.

The evidence has also unearthed a more compelling reason for the war than exists in the Epic Cycle. A city with Troy's affluence and strategic location would have created both the dedication required on the part of the Achaeans to take it and the investment in its defenses by the Trojans needed to keep it. Further, the later significance of Byzantium and even more recent battles of the First World War illustrate the militaristic importance of the site. Famously, over 130,000 soldiers died in the Battle of Gallipoli, a twentieth-century equivalent of Troy, geographically speaking. This importance would again support the necessity of an economically and militarily concentrated civilization that would have likely had many "Trojan Wars" in addition to the one fought against the Achaeans. This would mean that people had been fighting and dying over Troy for thousands of years before the Achaeans attacked it; who is to say if the Trojans of their time were themselves the original inhabitants or merely the most recent foreign conquerors?

If there was a Trojan War against the Achaeans, much of what has been previously assumed might be wrong. The war was probably not decided by a few important showdowns where one warrior called out another warrior. It was more likely the most recent series of skirmishes in a history of routine skirmishes with armies attempting to control the strategic city-state. There would have been fewer full-scale assaults than Homer described and more guerilla campaigns from each side: the Trojans against the Achaean encampments, and the Achaeans against the Trojan countryside. In short, it would have been more ugly than glorious. In a word, it would have been *just a war*.

Like many wars, it could have very well hinged on something tricky or clever that gave the Achaeans the edge at just the right time or caused the Trojans to let their guard down. It could have been something hatched by someone who resembled Odysseus, or it could have been the fatigue of war for the Trojans and good luck for the Greeks.

In the end, it is very tempting to believe as much as possible about Homer's Trojan War and its heroes, but it is just as dangerous as deifying any war effort. By putting it on the plain of virtue, its cancerous elements are swept under the rug to metastasize in our world as much as it did in theirs. Achilles is a fascinating character but would make a terrifying person. Worshiping someone like him is as much an appreciation of the human ability as it is to our tendency to forget the far greater number of "little people;" the civilians, peasants, and regular folk who all died in the name of his glory. In the end, this was at best a war about the honor of a handful of people, and at worst, *simply politics*. Heroism can always be displayed, but in response to – not as a cause of – war.

Did the face of Helen launch a thousand ships? Did the rage of Achilles kill a thousand people? The record tells us probably not, on both accounts and for different reasons. But there was very likely still a terrible war, with much senselessness and some heroism, though probably on the part of those who never sought it. The sad reality is that we're still asking the wrong questions.

What would we say of Helen if she were more than a marriage device? And what great deeds might Achilles have accomplished if not made a tool of Agamemnon? These questions put the war in its place as a hindrance to greater acts. Achilles would likely agree, as all he did in the end was to destroy other great warriors because it made him look good. Perhaps, though, the Greeks layered their myths deep, and this was *exactly* what Homer was saying. Achilles was not made great through the war; he was diminished by it. It consumed him and became him. He kept trying to leave (and wanting to leave) but kept getting drawn back by vanity and arrogance.

Remember, Achilles was one of the few heroes in Greek mythology who was given a choice.

Perhaps he chose against his better nature, ignoring his mother's advice, his own dislike of Agamemnon, and the independence he so desperately needed to assert by doing what everyone wanted and expected him to do. He had to have known that a talent for death was lonely, and a legacy of death was perhaps not very glorious of an achievement. Or maybe that is just transposing modern ideas onto a Bronze Age mind that had a very different moral code. Who is to say? The point is that the interpretations, symbolism, and meaning in Greek myths are as varied as the readers, *and that is exactly the reason why they persist.* Much like the Greek constellations, the unclear outlines are a feature, not a bug, and they allow people to see what they saw because of, *not in spite of,* their vagueness. Or something like it, anyway.

# Conclusion

Despite its many interpretations, thousands of class or research hours, and many archeological surprises supporting its assertion, Homer's *Iliad* remains one of the world's most-read and discussed works of all time. Though many would assess its importance from a historical perspective, an equal number of readers would likely draw its most important conclusions from a psychological standpoint.

Regardless of perspective, the Trojan War presented by Homer is still being debated from all angles today. This simple fact belies the continuing importance of understanding our past to assess our future.

Many historians posit that the Trojan War itself was not as important as the Homeric epic that followed, as the *Iliad* became somewhat of a Bible to the ancient Greeks. His account inspired thousands of people – not to mention the great warrior, Alexander the Great – and became one of the earliest and most-studied pieces of literature.

Still, history is not supported only by that one literary work. We have contemporary texts that support the fact that the Trojan War was not a small war – or one without significance. Mycenaean Greeks from much of the world united to attack Troy, garnering from 70,000 to possibly 130,000 men, traveling on an estimated 1,200 ships! This expedition was a huge undertaking for that time in history.

The fall of Troy likely triggered the Greek Dark Ages, lasting from about 1200 BCR to 800 BCE – no small occurrence in Greek history. Homer's *Iliad* was not only a recounting of a war story; it served as a unifying call for a rise from the ashes, clarity of purpose, and a patriotism that had all but been lost to the prior 400 years. The story – as told by Homer – helped the Greeks remember the myths and history of their past while also linking them to a common enemy during the period of the Persian Wars. In this way, the *Iliad* brought the past into their present, garnering national pride and a sense of destiny.

Notwithstanding that important influence, the Trojan War inspired the Greeks to invent the phonetic alphabet; they determined which vowels and consonants coexist to reproduce the sound of spoken words. Without this, the *Iliad* may not have been transformed from its oral story to its written form. Before this important time, cuneiform or pictographs were used for writing – and were unable to record human stories with power, majesty, and emotion. After all, the first word in Homer's epic poem? "Rage."

We would do well today to remember that apt word when approaching the potential for war.

# Here's another book by Enthralling History that you might like

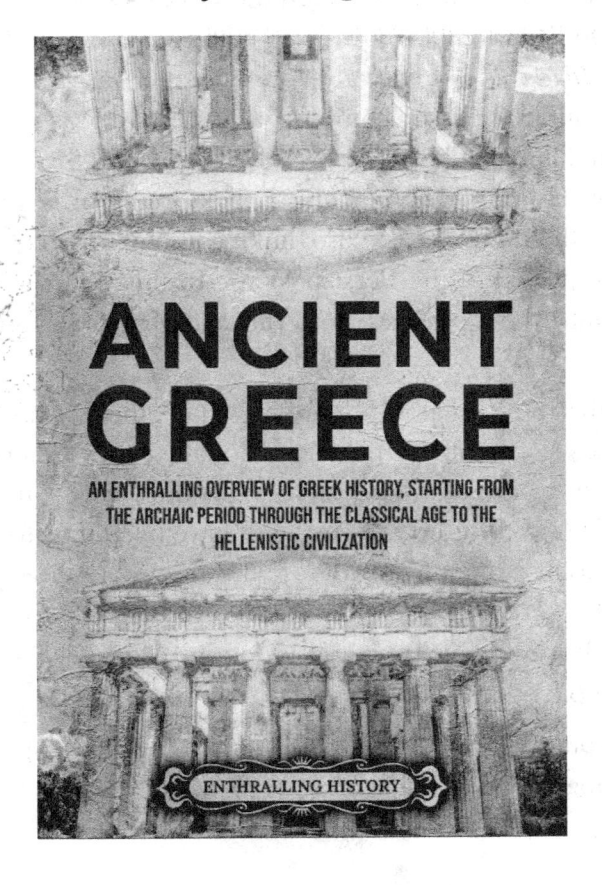

## ANCIENT GREECE

AN ENTHRALLING OVERVIEW OF GREEK HISTORY, STARTING FROM THE ARCHAIC PERIOD THROUGH THE CLASSICAL AGE TO THE HELLENISTIC CIVILIZATION

ENTHRALLING HISTORY

# Free limited time bonus

Stop for a moment. We have a free bonus set up for you. The problem is this: we forget 90% of everything that we read after 7 days. Crazy fact, right? Here's the solution: we've created a printable, 1-page pdf summary for this book that you're reading now. All you have to do to get your free pdf summary is to go to the following website: **https://livetolearn.lpages.co/enthrallinghistory/**

Once you do, it will be intuitive. Enjoy, and thank you!

# References

(2021). Retrieved 23 October 2021, from https://www.theoi.com/articles/what-was-the-cause-of-the-trojan-war/

(2021). Retrieved 23 October 2021, from https://www.greekmythology.com/Myths/Mortals/Philoctetes/philoctetes.html

(2021). Retrieved 23 October 2021, from https://www.greekmythology.com/Myths/Heroes/Achilles/achilles.html

(2021). Retrieved 23 October 2021, from https://www.greekmythology.com/Myths/Figures/Amazons/amazons.html#:~:text=The%20Amazons%20were%20a%20race,the%20god%20of%20war%20Ares.

(2021). Retrieved 23 October 2021, from https://www.masterclass.com/articles/writing-101-the-12-literary-archetypes#12-archetypal-characters-to-use-in-your-writing

(2021). Retrieved 23 October 2021, from https://www.baltimoresun.com/news/bs-xpm-1993-02-22-1993053194-story.html

Achaeans (Homer) - Wikipedia. (2021). Retrieved 23 October 2021, from https://en.wikipedia.org/wiki/Achaeans_(Homer)

Achilles - Wikipedia. (2021). Retrieved 23 October 2021, from https://en.wikipedia.org/wiki/Achilles#Death

Achilles | Myth, Meaning, Significance, & Trojan War. (2021). Retrieved 23 October 2021, from https://www.britannica.com/topic/Achilles-Greek-mythology

Aeneas - Wikipedia. (2021). Retrieved 23 October 2021, from https://en.wikipedia.org/wiki/Aeneas

Agamemnon - Wikipedia. (2021). Retrieved 23 October 2021, from https://en.wikipedia.org/wiki/Agamemnon

Amazon Warriors Did Indeed Fight and Die Like Men. (2021). Retrieved 23 October 2021, from https://www.nationalgeographic.com/history/article/141029-amazons-scythians-hunger-games-herodotus-ice-princess-tattoo-cannabis

Amazons - Wikipedia. (2021). Retrieved 23 October 2021, from https://en.wikipedia.org/wiki/Amazons

Ancient Troy: The City & the Legend. (2021). Retrieved 22 October 2021, from https://www.livescience.com/38191-ancient-troy.html

Apollo - Wikipedia. (2021). Retrieved 22 October 2021, from https://en.wikipedia.org/wiki/Apollo#Anatolian_origin

Brouwers, J. (2021). The suicide of Ajax. Retrieved 23 October 2021, from https://www.ancientworldmagazine.com/articles/suicide-ajax/

Cassandra - Wikipedia. (2021). Retrieved 22 October 2021, from https://en.wikipedia.org/wiki/Cassandra

Epic Cycle - Livius. (2021). Retrieved 23 October 2021, from https://www.livius.org/sources/content/epic-cycle/

Epic Cycle - The Center for Hellenic Studies. (2021). Retrieved 23 October 2021, from https://chs.harvard.edu/primary-source/epic-cycle-sb/

Epic Cycle - Wikipedia. (2021). Retrieved 23 October 2021, from https://en.wikipedia.org/wiki/Epic_Cycle

Expedition Magazine - Penn Museum. (2021). Retrieved 23 October 2021, from https://www.penn.museum/sites/expedition/the-hittites-and-the-aegean-world/

Fall of Troy: the legend and the facts. (2021). Retrieved 22 October 2021, from https://theconversation.com/fall-of-troy-the-legend-and-the-facts-92625

First Sacking of Troy in Greek Mythology. (2021). Retrieved 22 October 2021, from https://www.greeklegendsandmyths.com/first-sacking-of-troy.html

Geology corresponds with Homers description of ancient Troy. (2021). Retrieved 22 October 2021, from https://www1.udel.edu/PR/UDaily/2003/troy030303.html

Greek & Roman Mythology - Homer. (2021). Retrieved 23 October 2021, from https://www2.classics.upenn.edu/myth/php/homer/index.php?page=trojan

Hancox, D. (2021). The Archetypal Father. Retrieved 23 October 2021, from https://corecounselling.ca/the-archetypal-father/#:~:text=The%20Father%20archetype%20combines%20the,to%20put%20ideas%20into%20fruition.

Hector in Greek Mythology. (2021). Retrieved 22 October 2021, from https://www.greeklegendsandmyths.com/hector.html

Hercules' Ninth Labor: Hippolyte's Belt. (2021). Retrieved 23 October 2021, from http://www.perseus.tufts.edu/Heracles/amazon.html

Hippolyta in Greek Mythology. (2021). Retrieved 23 October 2021, from https://www.greeklegendsandmyths.com/hippolyta.html

Idomeneus of Crete - Wikipedia. (2021). Retrieved 23 October 2021, from https://en.wikipedia.org/wiki/Idomeneus_of_Crete

Iphigenia - Wikipedia. (2021). Retrieved 23 October 2021, from https://en.wikipedia.org/wiki/Iphigenia

Judgement of Paris - Wikipedia. (2021). Retrieved 23 October 2021, from https://en.wikipedia.org/wiki/Judgement_of_Paris

Lindberg, T. (2021). Achilles and Patroclus: Archetypal Heroes. Retrieved 23 October 2021, from https://warontherocks.com/2015/12/achilles-and-patroclus-archetypal-heroes/

Memnon: the African warrior who made Achilles bleed. (2021). Retrieved 23 October 2021, from https://thinkafrica.net/memnon-african-in-troy/

Menestheus - Wikipedia. (2021). Retrieved 23 October 2021, from https://en.wikipedia.org/wiki/Menestheus

Mike Greenberg, P., Mike Greenberg, P., & Mike Greenberg, P. (2021). Diomedes: A Hero of the Trojan War. Retrieved 23 October 2021, from https://mythologysource.com/diomedes-trojan-war/

Mycenaean Greece - Wikipedia. (2021). Retrieved 23 October 2021, from https://en.wikipedia.org/wiki/Mycenaean_Greece#Political_organization

Neill, C. (2021). Understanding Personality: The 12 Jungian Archetypes. Retrieved 23 October 2021, from https://conorneill.com/2018/04/21/understanding-personality-the-12-jungian-archetypes/

Nestor | Greek mythology. (2021). Retrieved 23 October 2021, from https://www.britannica.com/topic/Nestor-Greek-mythology

NPR Cookie Consent and Choices. (2021). Retrieved 23 October 2021, from https://www.npr.org/templates/story/story.php?storyId=6117459

Original Sources - Discover Trojan War. (2021). Retrieved 23 October 2021, from https://www.originalsources.com/Discover.aspx?ID=363

Original Sources - Fragment #1. (2021). Retrieved 23 October 2021, from https://www.originalsources.com/Document.aspx?DocID=SFSAGL8BJN6SDXM

Original Sources - Fragment #1. (2021). Retrieved 23 October 2021, from https://www.originalsources.com/Document.aspx?DocID=HNLSDCYI215BPWW

Original Sources - Fragment #1. (2021). Retrieved 23 October 2021, from https://www.originalsources.com/Document.aspx?DocID=CFYALH4C4RY16CA

Palladium (classical antiquity) - Wikipedia. (2021). Retrieved 23 October 2021, from https://en.wikipedia.org/wiki/Palladium_(classical_antiquity)

Peleus - Wikipedia. (2021). Retrieved 23 October 2021, from https://en.wikipedia.org/wiki/Peleus

Penthesilea. (2021). Retrieved 23 October 2021, from http://www.hellenicaworld.com/Greece/Mythology/en/Penthesilea.html

Philoctetes - Wikipedia. (2021). Retrieved 23 October 2021, from https://en.wikipedia.org/wiki/Philoctetes

Priam - Wikipedia. (2021). Retrieved 22 October 2021, from https://en.wikipedia.org/wiki/Priam

Scythians. (2021). Retrieved 23 October 2021, from https://www.worldhistory.org/Scythians/

Strauss, B. (2006). Strauss Offers Fresh Look at 'Trojan War'. Retrieved 22 October 2021, from https://www.npr.org/templates/story/story.php?storyId=6117459

Strauss, B. (2008). The Trojan War. London: Arrow.

The Final Labors of Heracles. (2021). Retrieved 23 October 2021, from https://www.greecetravel.com/greekmyths/argos8.htm

The Mythology of Tenedos. (2021). Retrieved 23 October 2021, from https://www.cointalk.com/threads/the-mythology-of-tenedos.332304/

The search for the lost city of Troy - British Museum Blog. (2021). Retrieved 23 October 2021, from https://blog.britishmuseum.org/the-search-for-the-lost-city-of-troy/

There could be surprising findings in Troy: Excavation head. (2021). Retrieved 22 October 2021, from https://www.hurriyetdailynews.com/there-could-be-surprising-findings-in-troy-excavation-head-136425

Thetis - More than Achilles's Mom. (2021). Retrieved 23 October 2021, from https://www.thoughtco.com/thetis-not-just-a-greek-nymph-116707

Trojan War - Wikipedia. (2021). Retrieved 23 October 2021, from https://en.wikipedia.org/wiki/Trojan_War#Gathering_of_Achaean_forces_and_the_first_expedition

Trojan War - Wikipedia. (2021). Retrieved 23 October 2021, from https://en.wikipedia.org/wiki/Trojan_War

Who Was Agamemnon? (2021). Retrieved 23 October 2021, from https://www.thoughtco.com/agamemnon-116781

Winkle, C. (2021). The Eight Character Archetypes of the Hero's Journey. Retrieved 23 October 2021, from https://mythcreants.com/blog/the-eight-character-archetypes-of-the-heros-journey/

Printed in Great Britain
by Amazon